TRIAD PARTICIPANT

The *Abba* JOURNEY

Drs. Kerry & Chiqui Wood

Unless otherwise noted, Scripture quotations are from the ESV® Bible (The Holy Bible, English Standard Version®), copyright © 2001 by Crossway, a publishing ministry of Good News Publishers. Used by permission. All rights reserved.

Scripture quotations marked NKJV are taken from the *New King James Version®* (NKJV). Copyright © 1982 by Thomas Nelson. Used by permission. All rights reserved.

Scripture quotations marked MSG are taken from *The Message.* Copyright © 1993, 1994, 1995, 1996, 2000, 2001, 2002 by Eugene H. Peterson.

Scripture quotations marked RSV are from *Revised Standard Version of the Bible,* copyright © 1946, 1952, and 1971 National Council of the Churches of Christ in the United States of America. Used by permission. All rights reserved worldwide.

Scripture quotations marked NEB taken from *the New English Bible,* copyright © Cambridge University Press and Oxford University Press 1961, 1970. All rights reserved.

Scripture quotations marked CEB taken from *the Common English Bible* copyright © The Common English Bible, Nashville, TN, All rights reserved.

Cover Design: Ivethe Zambrano-Fernández
wwwdesignbytwo.com

Photography of Author by John Choate

Bedford, Texas
www.BurkhartBooks.com

A Solid Foundation for
The *Abba* Journey

We have found that the optimal approach for personal transformation is in triads—three people studying, journeying, and growing together. An effective triad is comprised of three key components:

- **The presence of the Lord**, starting each triad meeting with worship and prayer,
- **The truth**, which comes through the content of the books,
- **Relationships**, which develops with and beyond your weekly time together.

In order to grow toward maturity in Christ, sonship to the Father, and partnership with the Spirit, the following ingredients are important to the foundation for our journey.

1. We commit ourselves to a relationship with (preferably) two others that will walk with us in humility, transparency, and diligence. That commitment includes an ongoing faithfulness to pray for one another, especially concerning those areas where need is expressed. The convener of the triad is a person who has been through *The Abba Journey* at least once.

2. We understand that accountability is only as good as the hearts and integrity of the participants. So we commit ourselves to one another in vulnerability, and confidentiality, asking the Lord to grace us to walk together.

3. We commit to approach the weekly "assignments" as encounter triggers—those ways that we best position ourselves to experience God's presence and word, far enough in advance of the weekly meeting that we have time to hear what the Spirit is saying. We understand that "just getting it done" is a violation of the spirit of waiting in the Father's presence in order to be transformed.

4. We commit to meet weekly with our partners for approximately 1 ½ hours to dialogue over the content of the week's assignment, minister to one another, and share what we are hearing from the Father.

5. We commit to offer ourselves fully to the Lord with the anticipation that we are entering a time of accelerated spiritual growth and learning new ways to commune with the Father, to hear His voice, and to partner with the Holy Spirit.

6. We also commit not only to see this journey through to the end (typically a 3-month process per section) but also to invest ourselves in at least two other people within a year of the initial completion of *The Abba Journey*. Part of the prayer focus will be to discern who needs to be discipled next.

7. In preparation for leading our own triads in the future, we commit to lead some of the triads in the last half of this journey as we are requested.

Introduction

The Importance of Significant Times in the Scriptures and Community

You may assume that such a powerful opportunity to accelerate your sonship-awareness would include good doses of the Scriptures, and so you should. But this is not naturally intuitive to an ever-increasing info-laden culture. As both pastors and professors, we have discovered that the newer generation of college student doesn't feel it is necessary to purchase their textbooks any more. Having grown up with Google, Siri, and Amazon Echo, the new assumption is, "Why should I have to read a book about it if I can just Google it?" This assumption is impacting our discipleship at a fundamental level. Eric Geiger writes about some paradoxes in our culture that we must both understand and respond to for the sake of spiritual transformation. Here are two of those paradoxes.

1. There is more information available but less learning.

Daniel Levitin, author of *The Organized Mind*, says "we have created more information in the last few years than all of human history before us."[1] We can browse articles on any subject, while being bombarded with snippets of information, and the general consumable knowledge is impossible to fathom, much less digest. We might think more information would mean more learning, but the opposite is the case. Geiger asserts that the national average SAT score has been on a declining trend for the last decade. The sad reality is that high school students read significantly less than they did in previous generations and the number of Americans who read works of literature is in decline.[2] More surfing and trolling with the smartphone has resulted in less deep reading, which equates to less critical thinking and deep learning. We can scan more subjects but experience less retention. More information is not creating more learning.

What does this mean for us? We must be intentionally engaging the Scriptures. Geiger says, "Sadly more information and less reading has the likelihood to impact spiritual formation among God's people." We cannot deny that God has used written words, the *graphe*, to encourage and instruct His people. God uses Scripture, not exclusively, but emphatically to save, train, and sanctify (2 Tim 3:16-17). Though we will promote the personal encounter with God, and the necessity of hearing the Father's voice for ourselves, we agree that the Bible is an indispensable element to spiritual growth.

---

[1] Daniel Levitin, *The Organized Mind: Thinking Straight in the Age of Information Overload.* Plume Pub, Random House, 2014.

[2] Eric Geiger. *Three Cultural Paradoxes Leaders Should Know and Respond To.* Twitter Post, April, 2018.

2. There is more connectivity but less community.

We can almost instantly connect with more people via the net, that at any other time in human history. One might scroll through dozens, even hundreds of messages from friends, acquaintances, Linked-in buddies or Insta-pals, but not actually have a conversation with more than a couple of people all day (depending upon work, station in life, etc.). This is a paradox. Rather than experiencing an increase of real community and the richness of sharing experiences this brings, the opposite is happening. Sherry Turkle, professor at MIT and author of *Alone Together,* articulates that we now live in the illusion of community without the demands for it. She says, "Instead of deep conversations and relationships, people often settle for casual connections. In our culture, people can easily be alone together instead of in community together."[3] The constant connectivity has given the illusion of community but has escalated loneliness and shallow relationships.

This is why *The Abba Journey* meets such a deep human need. Community must be facilitated. Fathers and mothers must bring the spiritual family together again. Why? Because God is first and foremost a relational being, and He has made a relational world. Doing community should be the forte of the Church. Believers must know and be known by one another—it's our love shared that gets the world's attention. Authentic community is even more important now as our culture is baptized in connectivity without commitment. Interestingly, the Church finds Herself standing as the only candle in the middle of a huge cake of humanity, with the greatest opportunity she has ever known to let her light so shine.

Please press in, even beyond your comfort level, to deeper reading (not just skimming) of the Scriptures. Read a passage several times. Learn to meditate upon the Scriptures until the Spirit breathes life into your spirit through the words. Press in to community, friendships, spending time with others and living in the moment. Especially if you consider yourself something of a loner or "the silent type." What if you are not? What if you have just believed a lie that you are a loner, and it isn't what God intended at all? What if your life is about to explode with fullness, fun, and new interests that you have never given a thought to before? Why wouldn't a good Heavenly Father want as much for His son or daughter? We simply ask you to ask Him to help you to press in a bit further.

---

[3]Sherry Turkle. *Alone Together: Why We Expect More from Technology and Less from Each Other.* Philadelphia: Perseus Books, 2011.

Instructions

Each week we will work through a chapter of *The Abba Trilogy*. This participant guide will walk you through several activities that you can do during the week in preparation for our time together. You can do these on your own time, but we suggest that you do a little bit each day. Don't wait until the day before the triad meeting to get started.

Each week will have the following components:

Meditation Verse

Context is important, so we're giving you a passage of Scripture to meditate upon, and the same verse in its context. The Meditation Verse is the theme for the chapter, so it will serve as a good reinforcement for the main idea. Read the verse in its context and meditate on it. Read it. Declare it. Think about its meaning. Write the verse on 3 x 5 cards, on as a Note on your phone so that you can pull it out several times a day, one verse each week. Put that one verse in your mouth, muttering to yourself, several times a day. This is not a mental exercise, this is a spiritual (*pneuma*) exercise. It is the only activity mentioned in the Bible that immediately connected to health and blessing (see Josh. 1:8; Ps. 1:1), but the most neglected activity in the Church. Ask God what He wants to say to you through it. Speak it out. The more you meditate on the verse, the more the Word becomes a fire in you—it comes alive. It will also make memorization automatic. For more details, you may want to jump ahead and study the Supplemental Article for week 8, "Daily Meditate on the Word."

Assigned Reading

This guide includes a summary of the assigned chapter to help you remember the most important themes, but the summary is not enough. It is necessary to read the assigned chapter from the book and answer the questions we provide for your reflection. To maximize our time together, think about highlighting other parts of the chapter that you want to discuss with your triad, such as areas where you need clarification or explanation, areas that are encouraging or challenging to you, or areas that you want to bring out into the open to invite the Lord to work in your life.

Supplemental Article

This article will address a related theme to help you go deeper in your walk with the Lord. Read it and use it as a starting point for a conversation with the Lord. Your triad discussion may include questions related to the article.

Personal Reflection

The last thing—and perhaps the most important one—is the section for you to record what the Lord is saying to you through this study. As you will see, hearing the voice of the Father is the primary catalyst for our transformation. So, take time to talk with Him. Use the reflection and prayer from the chapters as a starting point and write whatever you sense God is saying to you.

The *Abba* FOUNDATION

A disciple of Jesus is one
who freely receives the Father's love
and responds to His presence, evidenced
by other-centered love and action.

Week 1
A Matter of Perspective

Meditation Verse

> ***He who has seen Me has seen the Father. (John 14:9)***

The verse in context:

Jesus said to him, "I am the way, and the truth, and the life.
No one comes to the Father except through me. If you had known Me,
you would have known My Father also; and from now on you know
Him and have seen Him."

Philip said to Him, "Lord, show us the Father,
and it is sufficient for us."

Jesus said to him, "Have I been with you so long, and yet you have not
known Me, Philip? He who has seen Me has seen the Father; so how
can you say, 'Show us the Father?'"

John 14:6-9

Assigned Reading: *The Abba Foundation*, Chapter 1

Chapter Summary

What we believe about God determines what we believe about everything else. Unfortunately, our view of God has been formed by art, entertainment, music, religion, politics, and our own experiences. It has also been impacted by the Roman worldview, which focuses on law, rules and regulations; and by the Greek worldview, which emphasizes abstract thinking and a separation of the spiritual and material worlds. Neither of these values relationships; which is the focus of the Hebraic worldview that reflects most closely God's way of being. Another source that impacts our view of our Heavenly Father is our relationship with our earthly Father. All of these sources can result in a distorted view of the *Abba* of Jesus.

Jesus, however, is the express image of the Father. If we want to know *Abba*, we look to Jesus. Jesus is perfect theology. As simple as this sounds, knowing that Jesus is the highest revelation of the Father is significant for us. We can know God because Jesus has made Him known. This is good news!

A disciple of Jesus is one who freely receives the Father's love and responds to His presence, evidenced by other-centered love and action.

Questions:

1) Our view of God is influenced by many factors including art, entertainment, mythology, pop culture, politics, or religion. Can you think of a specific example of how we might perceive God based on <u>one</u> of these factors?

2) Our view of God is also influenced by life experiences. Describe an experience you have had that has shaped your view of God.

3) Our view of God (in the West) has been shaped by Roman and Greek views. Take an honest assessment of your view of God and explain whether it is more Roman, Greek, or Hebrew.

4) Describe your earthly father. How has your experience with him shaped your view of God (positively or negatively)?

A disciple of Jesus is one who freely receives the Father's love and responds to His presence, evidenced by other-centered love and action.

12

5) There are several examples that show the implication that "if Jesus didn't do it, the Father won't do it, either." Select one that stands out to you and describe how seeing Jesus as the "express image of the Father" reframe your perspective on God's way of being.

6) God wants us to *know* Him. Discuss how you get to know somebody. If you were making a new friend, what would you do to get to know him better? What would you do to find out how he thinks or what he likes?

· ·

Supplemental Article

Encounter Triggers
—Learning to Value the Voice of God

We were made for the presence of God. Our spirits thrive in our Father's presence. When it's all said and done, the verifiable difference between those that know God and those that don't, is the practice of His presence. In His presence is fullness—of righteousness, peace, and joy in the Holy Spirit. Our hearts are at home there, though our minds feel a bit of a loss of control. We have too often settled for a weekly worship service as though we still live in the Old Testament, needing to make our way to the Temple, when His presence (by the indwelling Holy Spirit) has taken up His home in us. We are to cultivate the presence of God up from our spirits into our environment by singing songs, hymns, spiritual songs, making melody from our hearts to the Lord (Col. 3:16; Eph. 5:16-18).

Historically, this welcoming, inviting, practicing the presence of God has been called spiritual disciplines. But as often happens in spiritual things, what some discover as a path to a grand revelation, only becomes a picture postcard to someone else. The spiritual disciplines that once brought life are reduced, in the next generation, to a "to do list" at best, or a set of religious rules at the worst.

A disciple of Jesus is one who freely receives the Father's love and responds to His presence, evidenced by other-centered love and action.

But what if spiritual disciplines are really doorways through which we release the presence of God that is already in us? What if these spiritual pathways are not really about "getting closer to God" (as though God was happy with some distance), but about becoming more aware of who we really are and living in that conscious reality? What if prayer, worship, feeding on the Scriptures, fellowship with one another, communion, and even fasting, were not actually about trying to get closer to God, but ways in which we cultivate (stir up) His presence so that we can give it away?

If we begin to understand spiritual disciplines as "encounter triggers" whereby we meet God by the indwelling presence of the Spirit, then we are not twisting God's arm for an answer, we are immersing ourselves in who He is. And this is what I know: the surest way and most direct path of transformation from an orphan spirit to sonship (see The Abba Factor), is to hear the Father's voice (by the Spirit). We know that the Father is always speaking His love to us. Jesus said, "Man will not live by bread alone, but by every word which comes [is continually proceeding] from the mouth of God" (Matt. 4:4). Spiritual disciplines are simply positioning ourselves to hear the Father speak to us, "You are my beloved son/daughter; in you I am well pleased."

Much has been said and written about practicing the presence of God. Suffice it to say here that it is difficult to conceive of any believer that walks in a revelation of the reality of their sonship that does not learn the importance of the abiding presence of God. It is by that abiding presence that Jesus did what He did (Acts 10:38), and that we are empowered as sons to do "these same works" (John 14:12-14).

As we read the chapter each week, process the Scripture passage, meditate upon a verse of Scripture, please keep this question at the forefront: "Father, what are you saying to me today through this? Holy Spirit, speak to me. I am listening. I position myself right now—I quieten my busy mind to hear Your voice in my spirit." Then get in the habit of writing down what you sense, hear, feel, or see. God will speak more and more clearly as you value His words more and more.

A disciple of Jesus is one who freely receives the Father's love and responds to His presence, evidenced by other-centered love and action.

Personal Reflection

What is the Lord saying to you?

*A disciple of Jesus is one who freely receives the Father's love and responds to His
presence, evidenced by other-centered love and action.*

15

A disciple of Jesus is one who freely receives the Father's love and responds to His presence, evidenced by other-centered love and action.

16

Week 2
Our Relational God

Meditation Verse

> *I pray for them, that they all may be one, as You, Father,
> are in Me, and I in You; that they also may be one in Us,
> that the world may believe that You sent Me. (John 17:21)*

The verse in context:

> *"I do not ask for these only, but also for those who will believe in me
> through their word, that they may all be one, just as you, Father, are
> in me, and I in you, that they also may be in us, so that the world may
> believe that you have sent me. The glory that you have given me I have
> given to them, that they may be one even as we are one, I in them and
> you in me, that they may become perfectly one, so that the world may
> know that you sent me and loved them even as you loved me."*
>
> John 17:20-23

Assigned Reading: *The Abba Foundation*, Chapter 2

Chapter Summary

God has existed eternally in a relationship of love and mutual self-giving.
This is what we call the Trinity. The Trinity is the community created by our
Heavenly Father, Jesus the Son, and the Holy Spirit. God is three persons, one
essence; all eternal, fully equal, but fully distinct. God's way of being is *ekstasis*:
always "going out" in an overflow of infinite, personal, communal, and self-
giving love. The quality of life of the Trinity is the *perichoresis*, which can be
described as a circle dance of shared love, mutual other-centeredness and self-
giving, perfect harmony, joy, peace, affirmation, and acceptance.

If God is in fact first and foremost relational, then it follows that everything
that God does is consistent with His relational way of being. The Father's
creation, His will, His mission, His expectations and desires for you, His
commandments, all flow out of His love.

God is not an angry, reluctant deity in need of appeasement—as we often
think He is. God is a zealous lover, yearning to share who He is with His
creation. Maybe He is not as interested in you learning to keep certain rules,
or developing a good ethical and moral lifestyle as He is in you experiencing
fullness of life.

---

*A disciple of Jesus is one who freely receives the Father's love and responds to His
presence, evidenced by other-centered love and action.*

Questions:

1) How is our God different from the gods of other religions?

2) Why is it important for us to know that God is three-in-one?

3) How does knowing God as a relational, loving, other-centered, "being in relationship" who "can't keep Himself to Himself" impact your view of Him?

4) Have you ever thought of how Father, Son, and Holy Spirit relate to one another? What would their conversation sound like?

A disciple of Jesus is one who freely receives the Father's love and responds to His presence, evidenced by other-centered love and action.

18

5) In John 17:20-23 Jesus expresses His desire that we may be one as He and the Father are one. What does it mean to be "one" as they are one?

6) What would our family, church and/or community look like if we would live as a community of persons who participate in *perichoresis* (the relational wholeness of the Father, Son, and Holy Spirit)?

• •

Supplemental Article

The Rabbi's Gift
(Author unknown)

The story concerns a monastery that had fallen upon hard times. It was once a great order, but because of persecution, all its branch houses were lost and there were only five monks left in the decaying house: the Abbot and four others, all over seventy in age. Clearly it was a dying order.

In the deep woods surrounding the monastery there was a little hut that a Rabbi occasionally used for a hermitage. It occurred to the Abbot that a visit the Rabbi might result in some advice to save his monastery. The Rabbi welcomed the Abbot to his hut. But when the Abbot explained his visit, all the Rabbi could say was, "I know how it is. The spirit has gone out of the people. It is the same in my town. Almost no one comes to the synagogue anymore." So the old Abbot and the old Rabbi wept together. Then they read parts of the Torah and spoke of deep things. When the Abbot had to leave, they embraced each other. "It has been a wonderful that we should meet after all these years," the Abbot said, "but I have failed in my purpose for coming here. Is there nothing you can tell me that would help me save my dying order?"

"No, I am sorry," the Rabbi responded. "I have no advice to give. But, I can tell you that the Messiah is one of you."

A disciple of Jesus is one who freely receives the Father's love and responds to His presence, evidenced by other-centered love and action.

When the Abbot returned to the monastery his fellow monks gathered around him to ask,

"Well what did the Rabbi say?"

"The Rabbi said something very mysterious, it was something cryptic. He said that the Messiah is one of us. I don't know what he meant."

In the time that followed, the old monks pondered the significance to the Rabbi's words. The Messiah is one of us? Could he possibly have meant one of us monks? If so, which one?

Do you suppose he meant the Abbot? Yes, if he meant anyone, he probably meant Father Abbot. He has been our leader for more than a generation. On the other hand, he might have meant Brother Thomas. Certainly Brother Thomas is a holy man. Everyone knows that Thomas is a man of light. Certainly he could not have meant Brother Mark! Mark gets crotchety at times. But come to think of it, even though he is a thorn in people's sides, when you look back on it, Mark is virtually always right. Often very right. Maybe the Rabbi did mean Brother Mark. But surely not Brother Phillip. Phillip is so passive, a real nobody. But then, almost mysteriously, he has a gift for always being there when you need him. He just magically appears. Maybe Phillip is the Messiah.

Of course the Rabbi didn't mean me. He couldn't possibly have meant me. I'm just an ordinary person. Yet supposing he did? Suppose I am the Messiah? O God, not me. I couldn't be that much for You, could I?

As they contemplated, the old monks began to treat each other with extraordinary respect on the chance that one among them might be the Messiah. And they began to treat themselves with extraordinary respect.

People still occasionally came to visit the monastery in its beautiful forest to picnic on its tiny lawn, to wander along some of its paths, even to meditate in the dilapidated chapel. As they did so, they sensed the aura of extraordinary respect that began to surround the five old monks and seemed to radiate out from them and permeate the atmosphere of the place. There was something strangely compelling, about it. Hardly knowing why, they began to come back to the monastery to picnic, to play, to pray. They brought their friends to this special place. And their friends brought their friends.

Then some of the younger men who came to visit the monastery started to talk more and more with the old monks. After a while one asked if he could join them. Then another, and another. So within a few years the monastery had once again become a thriving order and, thanks to the Rabbi's gift, a vibrant center of light and spirituality in the realm.

A disciple of Jesus is one who freely receives the Father's love and responds to His presence, evidenced by other-centered love and action.

Personal Reflection

What is the Lord saying to you?

A disciple of Jesus is one who freely receives the Father's love and responds to His presence, evidenced by other-centered love and action.

21

A disciple of Jesus is one who freely receives the Father's love and responds to His presence, evidenced by other-centered love and action.

22

Week 3
The Father and Creation

Meditation Verse

Let us make man in our image, after our likeness. (Genesis 1:26)

The verse in context:

> *Then God said, "Let us make man in our image, after our likeness. And let them have dominion over the fish of the sea and over the birds of the heavens and over the livestock and over all the earth and over every creeping thing that creeps on the earth." So God created man in his own image, in the image of God he created him; male and female he created them. And God blessed them. And God said to them, "Be fruitful and multiply and fill the earth and subdue it, and have dominion over the fish of the sea and over the birds of the heavens and over every living thing that moves on the earth."*
>
> Genesis 1:26-28

Assigned Reading: *The Abba Foundation*, Chapter 3

Chapter Summary

God doesn't create out of necessity or compulsion. He creates, not because He needs to, but because He wants to. Since God's way of being is *ekstasis*—outgoing, self-giving love—God can't keep it to himself, so the act of creation naturally flows out of God's overflowing love way of being. By looking at the Genesis account we can see that God delights in His creation, and especially in the creation of humanity— male and female—made in His image and likeness, and created for the purpose of relationship and partnership.

God delights in who you are, simply because you are His. You didn't do anything to deserve God's love; and therefore, there is nothing you can do to keep Father, Son, and Holy Spirit from loving you.

Humans, created in the *Imago Dei,* are relational by nature. Contrary to what our individualistic culture may promote, we enjoy full personhood only in the context of relationships. Our significance comes when we see that others have need of who we are and what we have to give. Because we are made in the image of God, as we know God, we come to know ourselves and one another better; and as we know one another, we know God better.

A disciple of Jesus is one who freely receives the Father's love and responds to His presence, evidenced by other-centered love and action.

23

Questions:

1) If God created not out of necessity, but out of love, through love, and for love, what does that say about why He created you?

2) What do you think about God's declaration: "*towb meod*" when He created humanity?

3) If God is relational, and we are made in His image (*Imago Dei*), what does that say about His purposes for us?

4) Give an example of how the fullness of who you are is expressed when you have others with whom you can share your gifts.

5) How does individualism hinder us from experiencing the fullness of life that the Father intends for us? What can you do, specifically, to cultivate more meaningful relationships?

A disciple of Jesus is one who freely receives the Father's love and responds to His presence, evidenced by other-centered love and action.

Supplemental Article

Carriers of God's Glory

1 Kings 6 describes the temple that Solomon built. It is quite an impressive structure, with great attention to detail, and the "best of the best." It is massive, built with quality stones, cedar wood, all kinds of carving, and overlaid with gold.

In my mind I picture this and think of the churches and cathedrals I have visited that take my breath away. The massive structures, with beautiful stained-glass windows, lots of gold, gems and artwork. They are so ornate …

Then I think, Why? Why would we build such ornate, lavish structures?

Because they are temples, fit for a King—and not just any King, but the King of kings. The buildings display, in human terms, the splendor and majesty of the King. It seems that the goal is to evoke a sense of awe and wonder for the glory of the King.

And yet … I am reminded that the glory of our King is magnificently displayed in the person of Jesus—in God the almighty, the King of kings, taking human form—the lowliest of lowlies, the servant of all. Certainly our King is not like earthly kings. His glory is beyond our comprehension. In Jesus, He has chosen to forever have humanity be the temple of His glory.

Look at what Paul says in Acts 17:24-25:

The God who made the world and everything in it, being Lord of heaven and earth, does not live in temples made by man, nor is he served by human hands, as though he needed anything, since he himself gives to all mankind life and breath and everything.

Then in 1 Corinthians 6:19 he reminds us:

Do you not know that your body is a temple of the Holy Spirit within you, whom you have from God?

Our King is crowned in glory and majesty. And … WOW! … could it be that His glory is in me?

In Ephesians 1:15-18, Paul prays for us:

For this reason … I do not cease to give thanks for you, remembering you in my prayers, that the God of our Lord Jesus Christ, the Father of glory, may give you the Spirit of wisdom and of revelation in the knowledge of him, having the eyes of your hearts

A disciple of Jesus is one who freely receives the Father's love and responds to His presence, evidenced by other-centered love and action.

25

enlightened, that you may know what is the hope to which he has called you, what are the riches of his glorious inheritance in the saints.

Did you catch that? We need a Spirit of wisdom and revelation to know the riches of His glorious inheritance IN the saints ... Not FOR the saints, but IN the saints.

We are His glorious inheritance. The scandal of the Gospel is that our King has chosen for His glory to show through the imperfection of human vessels.

You are a carrier of His glory! His power is made perfect in your weakness. Wherever you go, let His glory shine in your life. Let Him be through you. Let others see His splendor when they see you. Let others be touched by His majesty when they come in contact with you. You are a carrier of God's glory!

. . . .

Personal Reflection

What is the Lord saying to you?

A disciple of Jesus is one who freely receives the Father's love and responds to His presence, evidenced by other-centered love and action.

Week 4
The Father's Will

Meditation Verse

> *Truly, truly, I say to you, the Son can do nothing of his own accord, but only what he sees the Father doing. For whatever the Father does, that the Son does likewise. (John 5:19)*

The verse in context:

> *So Jesus said to them, "Truly, truly, I say to you, the Son can do nothing of his own accord, but only what he sees the Father doing.*
> *For whatever the Father does, that the Son does likewise.*
> *For the Father loves the Son and shows him all that he himself is doing. And greater works than these will he show him, so that you may marvel. For as the Father raises the dead and gives them life, so also the Son gives life to whom he will. For the Father judges no one, but has given all judgment to the Son, that all may honor the Son, just as they honor the Father. Whoever does not honor the Son does not honor the Father who sent him. Truly, truly, I say to you, whoever hears my word and believes him who sent me has eternal life. He does not come into judgment, but has passed from death to life.*
>
> John 5:19-24

Assigned Reading: *The Abba Foundation*, Chapter 4

Chapter Summary

Even though God created a "very good" world, there are many things that happen—both in the big scheme of things and in our personal lives—that aren't good. These aren't the Father's will. Not everything that happens is God's will; and God's will is not always done on earth. Bad things happen because of (a) Satan's direct attack, (b) the exercise of our free will, or (c) because we live in a broken world and suffer the effects of the cumulative effect to humanity's sin.

Even though God is sovereign and could do something about the evil in our world, His love is such that He allows us to exercise our free will without His intervention. Said another way, in His sovereignty, God chose to limit Himself to protect our freewill for the purpose of relationship—at great cost to Himself.

A disciple of Jesus is one who freely receives the Father's love and responds to His presence, evidenced by other-centered love and action.

God wants for His will to be done on earth but has chosen to limit Himself to human cooperation, so we have the privilege of partnering with God—in prayer and action—for His will to be established on earth. We must understand that *Abba* is not passive about the brokenness in the world. He is doing something about it.

Questions:

1) Have you heard people refer to hurricanes, tornadoes, earthquakes, or the like as "acts of God"? Discuss the implication of seeing these destructive events as acts of God. What happens to our faith when we see God as both creator and destroyer of His creation?

2) Can you think of a situation where you (or a loved one) experienced pain and thought it was God's doing? How does this chapter help you discern God's will in the situation?

3) Can you think of a time when you (or a loved one) experienced pain as a consequence of your own (or someone else's) free will choices? How does this chapter help you understand the Father's will in that situation?

4) Can you think of a time when you experienced brokenness as a consequence of the cumulative effect of humanity's sin? How does this chapter help you discern God's will in those situations?

A disciple of Jesus is one who freely receives the Father's love and responds to His presence, evidenced by other-centered love and action.

28

5) Based on what we covered in this chapter can you think of ways to explain to someone else the fact that God loves us so much that He allows bad things to happen?

- -

Supplemental Article

From Old to New

Keeping the Great Divide in View

It's been said that the Old Testament is the New Testament concealed, and the New Testament is the Old Testament revealed. This speaks to the fact that these two belong together, and are both valuable, but have a distinction of purpose. The Old is written for our example and admonition (1 Cor. 10:11). But the seeming harshness of the Old Testament can be confusing to believers.

No matter how long we have been walking with the Lord, when reading the Old Testament, we can sometimes feel disoriented, as if stepping into in a foreign world, a foreign language, and a God that is barely recognizable to the New Testament. Anyone who uses a One Year Bible and reads a portion from the Old, a portion from the New, and a passage from Psalms each day, will notice this stark distinction repeatedly. It may lead us to ask, "Is God different in the Old Testament than the New?" The answer is "No!" God doesn't change. But in His gracious love, He reveals himself slowly, little by little, in ways people can understand.

Understanding God's Progressive Self-revelation:

- **God meets us where we are.** Adam and Eve sinned, God isn't the one hiding. Humans hide; God comes calling. We must acknowledge that God is the one who reaches out for us. He lowers Himself, comes into our world, and speaks to us in our language. One example we've used is that of God asking Abraham to offer his only son on Mt. Moriah. That wasn't unusual for Abraham; that's what all the Chaldean worshippers of Molech did. God was speaking Abraham's language. What was radically new was not only that God provided His own sacrifice, but

A disciple of Jesus is one who freely receives the Father's love and responds to His presence, evidenced by other-centered love and action.

that He revealed Himself in a new way—Jehovah Jireh, the Lord that Provides, completely different from all other gods. God has always been willing to limit His revelation to what we could understand at the time.

- **The Old Testament world was very different from our own.** Similar to the story of Abraham and Isaac, we read stories of divinely commanded genocide (entire cities wiped out by God's command), or David as a terrorist raiding cities and villages and taking the plunder (1 Sam. 27:8; 2 Sam. 3:22). We cannot fathom how a good God would condone such actions. What we need to understand through the "express image" of Jesus (which came in "the fullness of times") is that, even though this was not God's best for them, it was the way of the world. It was normal to them, even if abhorrent to God. It would have been too great a leap for them, in that context, to understand Jesus' admonition to "love your enemies." But in His patience and mercy, He worked with them in their context, revealing His will little by little, biding time until He could bring a clearer representation of Himself.

- **The Old Testament is never the final word.** When we read from the Old Testament, we must be asking, "Where is the Story going?" The answer is always: Jesus. The Old Testament is about 80% narrative. God is the hero of every story, and Jesus is the final scene. But like any narrative, you cannot draw a conclusion of the story in the middle or first few chapters of the book. It must unfold. The final act of this play is Jesus, the Word who became flesh, who redeems all things back to God—because by Him, for Him, and through Him are all things made. Don't draw any conclusions about God until Jesus comes on the scene and reveals God for who He really is (John 14:6-9).

The Jewish people came up with a "credo of five adjectives" to describe the God they met on their journey. YHWH was merciful, gracious, faithful, forgiving, and steadfast in love[4] You must realize what a breakthrough that was in human history and how it allowed one such as Jesus to emerge from such a worldview. The Barbaric cultures of the ancient era saw a graciousness they had never known before, but even that looks sadistic when contrasted to the kind of lavish lovingkindness

---

[4]Walter Brueggemann, *Theology of the Old Testament*. (Fortress Press, 1997), 216.

A disciple of Jesus is one who freely receives the Father's love and responds to His presence, evidenced by other-centered love and action.

demonstrating in the face of Jesus Christ. For this reason, it's important that we keep the differences in view between the Old and New Covenants:

Key Verse:

> *"I will give you a new heart and put a new spirit within you; I will take the heart of stone out of your flesh and give you a heart of flesh. I will put My Spirit within you and cause you to walk in My statutes, and you will keep My judgments and do them."*
> Ezek. 36:26-27

In the Old Testament:

- No one was "saved/born again" yet. Their hearts were stony, evil hearts (Jer. 16:11-12; Ezek. 36:26-27).
- Their nature was spiritual death (John 6:53; Eph. 2:1-2; Rom. 3:9-20).
- Their spiritual father was the devil [though they had a covenant with God] (John 8:44).
- Their minds and hearts were blinded; no revelation (1 Cor. 2:9; Is. 64:4).
- Old Testament prayers included revenge and murder (Ps. 139:19).

In the New Testament (after the death/resurrection of Christ), "A New Creation in Christ:"

- Everyone has the possibility, through Christ, of a new heart, a clean conscience, (2 Cor. 5:17; Heb. 9:14).
- The new nature is life, alive to God in new way (Eph. 2:1; Rom. 6:11,13; John 20:31).
- Our Father is God (John 20:17; Rom. 1:7; 15:6; 1 Cor. 1:3; 2 Cor. 1:2-3; Gal. 1:3; Eph. 1:2-3).
- God reveals by the Spirit had been hidden before (1 Cor. 2:10).
- New Testament prayers aren't for vengeance or judgment on others, but blessing (Matt. 5:44).

We cannot underestimate the two great watershed moments of Human history (both in Jesus):

- The Incarnation. God become human (fully God, fully Man) in Christ.
- The Cross. Jesus so identified (in oneness) with mankind that He took our judgment (2 Cor. 5:21).

What we have (internally) that Old Testament saints didn't have:

- The power that raised Jesus from the dead is at work within you (Eph. 1:19-20).
- The word that brings life (not death) works in you (1 Thess. 2:13).

A disciple of Jesus is one who freely receives the Father's love and responds to His presence, evidenced by other-centered love and action.

- The Father is working in you through Jesus Christ (Heb. 13:20-21).
- Eternal life is at work in you (2 Cor. 4:12; 1 John 5:11-12).
- The Holy Spirit dwells in you and gives life (Rom. 8:9, 11; 2 Cor. 3:16; 2 Tim. 1:14).
- The anointing abides in you and teaches you all things (1 John 2:27).

Remember This:

Only God is Good (Mark 10:18). God is not good sometimes and bad sometimes. He doesn't do good things sometimes and bad things sometimes. All goodness is measured by Him. We just haven't seen Him on full display until Jesus came as "the express image" of the Father.

So, you might say, "Why should I read the Old Testament at all?" We have said that the Old Testament Scriptures were written for our instruction and as examples, but not written directly to us. That is not to say that there are not treasure-loads of truth, instruction, and wisdom as we watch God graciously deal with fallen humanity.

In the Old Testament:

- We should note how patient is our loving God, slowly lifting humanity, until the fullness of times when God can bring forth His Son to demonstrate power in compassion, not wrath.
- We should note how jealous God is for our love and focused affection (No idolatry).
- We should note the outcome of disobedience (pain and sorrow which God never intended).
- We should understand that no man could keep the Law (without the indwelling Spirit); in fact, the Law was never intended to save, but to point Israel/mankind to the need of a Savior.
- We should also see that this loving Father is awesome beyond comprehension and to be reverenced. Our *Abba* Father is fearfully awesome and not to be taken lightly.

Conclusion:

Finally, you will live the rest of your life in the tension between the Old Testament and the New. If you will keep these distinctions in your mind as you toggle back and forth between the two Testaments, you will understand God did not expect them to hear and understand fully, until they could be regenerated in spirit, the eyes of their heart flooded with light (Eph. 1:17-18). You will also avoid the snare of trying to understand God through the lens of the Old Testament (as beautiful as it is), when He has given us the high definition view,

A disciple of Jesus is one who freely receives the Father's love and responds to His presence, evidenced by other-centered love and action.

"the face of Jesus Christ" (2 Cor 3:16, 27) to see Him clearly. When you read Old Testament stories that seem unjust, bloody, chauvinistic, or heartless, you will ask yourself, "Where is the story going? Oh yes, Jesus hasn't come on the scene yet. The Hero is on His way. For what the New Testament reveals is what the Old Testament only hinted at:

> *For by Him [Jesus Christ]*
> *all things were created*
> *that are in heaven and*
> *that are on earth, visible*
> *and invisible, whether*
> *thrones or dominions or*
> *principalities or powers.*
> *All things were created*
> *through Him and for Him*
> *... and by Him [the Father]*
> *reconciles all things to*
> *Himself, whether things on*
> *earth or things in heaven,*
> *having made peace through*
> *the blood of His cross ....*
> *For it was fitting for Him,*
> *for whom are all things and*
> *by whom are all things, in*
> *bringing many sons*
> *to glory, to make the*
> *captain of their salvation*
> *perfect through sufferings.*
> Col. 1:16, 20; Heb. 2:10

• •

Personal Reflection

What is the Lord saying to you?

A disciple of Jesus is one who freely receives the Father's love and responds to His
presence, evidenced by other-centered love and action.

A disciple of Jesus is one who freely receives the Father's love and responds to His presence, evidenced by other-centered love and action.

34

Week 5
The Father's Mission

Meditation Verse

> *For God did not send his Son into the world to condemn the world, but in order that the world might be saved through him. (John 3:17)*

The verse in context:

> *No one has ascended into heaven except he who descended from heaven, the Son of Man. And as Moses lifted up the serpent in the wilderness, so must the Son of Man be lifted up, that whoever believes in him may have eternal life. For God so loved the world, that he gave his only Son, that whoever believes in him should not perish but have eternal life. For God did not send his Son into the world to condemn the world, but in order that the world might be saved through him. Whoever believes in him is not condemned, but whoever does not believe is condemned already, because he has not believed in the name of the only Son of God.*
>
> John 3:13-18

Assigned Reading: *The Abba Foundation*, Chapter 5

Chapter Summary

We have seen that the brokenness we see around us is not the Father's will; but creation is broken, nonetheless. Therefore, the Father wants to restore broken Creation back to His original intent. To understand salvation, we must first understand that "sin" goes much deeper than simply bad behavior. The Father is not content to leave us in our brokenness. He has done something about it!

Jesus establishes clearly that *Abba* is not intent on condemning the world, but on saving it. This means that God wants to protect, deliver, and restore us. Jesus' mission clearly shows a loving, tender God who identifies with our weakness and gives us hope. He loves us so much that He became one of us—the incarnate Son: Jesus—to set us free from the destructive patterns of our world.

Jesus bore all the consequences of our sin, once and for all, to make us whole—whole in our being, whole in our relationship with Him, and whole in

---

A disciple of Jesus is one who freely receives the Father's love and responds to His presence, evidenced by other-centered love and action.

our relationships with one another. By believing in Him, we don't have to live a perishing, broken existence; instead we can experience fullness of life as the Father, Son, and Holy Spirit have it. This is eternal life: the God-kind of life, characterized by perfect union and harmony, abundance of love, joy, peace, affirmation, and acceptance. This is the kind of life that Jesus makes available to us—in the here and now. This is the Father's mission, and it's good news! This is the essence of the Gospel, and God invites us to partake of His free gift. He wants us to live in the wholeness that He has made possible for us, so He calls us to live holy lives.

Questions:

1) What is the meaning of "salvation" (sōzō) and why is it important for us to know that it's more than "a ticket to Heaven?"

2) Reflect on the characteristics of Jesus' mission. Which one stands out to you? Why?

3) Refer to the explanation of John 3:16 (The Promise of Eternal Life). What stands out to you? Why?

A disciple of Jesus is one who freely receives the Father's love and responds to His presence, evidenced by other-centered love and action.

4) Based on the Scriptures discussed in this chapter how would you explain the Father's mission to someone else?

5) A frequent question in the Church is whether someone can lose his/her salvation. Based on what we have seen of the Father's mission, how would you respond to that? (Remember how we define "salvation").

• •

Supplemental Article

The Problem with Being "Followers of Jesus"

It is common to think about Christianity about "following Jesus." And Jesus, of course, is the best model to follow because He lived a sinless life. He is the greatest teacher that ever lived; He gave us the "golden rule." So, certainly, the world would be a much better place if everyone followed Jesus.

How is this different than the claims of the Buddhists who want to follow Buddha, or the Muslims who follow their prophet and the teachings of Allah? Or Hindus who strive to live "good lives?"

You see, all religions have this in common: the goal is to live better lives, to be loving, kind, and compassionate to one another. We are all after "world peace," and there are certainly many ideas and

opinions as to the best way to reach that goal. If that is the case, then the Universalists have it right— just choose the path that works for you because, at the end of the day, we are all headed toward the same goal. Right?

OK. Don't shoot me yet ... I'm going somewhere.

I know there is a VAST difference between Christianity and every other religion in the world. But at face value, if all the world is hearing from us is that we need to be "followers of Jesus," then they are right in assessing that Christianity is just one among many options.

But being a Christian is not about imitating the actions of Jesus. It is about being born again,

A disciple of Jesus is one who freely receives the Father's love and responds to His presence, evidenced by other-centered love and action.

born of the Spirit. It is about our nature being changed, our spirit being made alive again by the Holy Spirit, so that, as Paul says, "it is no longer I who lives, but Christ lives in me."

You can imitate Jesus all day long—even study the Bible and endeavor to follow all of its principles and precepts; but if you are not born of the Spirit, you are not a Christian. You do not have eternal life.

Notice that the Bible says that God "anointed Jesus with the Holy Spirit and power, who went about doing good and healing all who were oppressed of the devil, for God was with Him." So, you want to be a follower of Jesus? Then you need to be anointed with the Holy Spirit and with power.

Salvation is more than an assent to a moral or ethical code; it is a supernatural event, initiated by God, of which we can partake by receiving what He has done for us. We accept His gift and receive the Holy Spirit and then, only then, are we saved. And the, as sons and daughters of God, we can live a radically different life—a life of partnership in the Father's mission, by the Son, in the power of the Holy Spirit.

The world needs to see a supernatural Church—a Church that moves in the power of the Holy Spirit; a Church that doesn't point an accusing finger to those enslaved by sin, but that proclaims God's compassion and healing to the broken and the outcast. If we are to imitate Jesus, let's be filled with the Spirit and do the works of the Father. If we are to imitate Jesus, let it be in the supernatural expression of God's compassion.

· ·

Personal Reflection

What is the Lord saying to you?

A disciple of Jesus is one who freely receives the Father's love and responds to His presence, evidenced by other-centered love and action.

Week 6
The Father and Holiness

Meditation Verse

> *You therefore must be perfect, as your heavenly Father is perfect. (Matthew 5:48)*

The verse in context:

> *You have heard that it was said, 'You shall love your neighbor and hate your enemy.' But I say to you, Love your enemies and pray for those who persecute you, so that you may be sons of your Father who is in heaven. For he makes his sun rise on the evil and on the good, and sends rain on the just and on the unjust. For if you love those who love you, what reward do you have? Do not even the tax collectors do the same? And if you greet only your brothers, what more are you doing than others? Do not even the Gentiles do the same? You therefore must be perfect, as your heavenly Father is perfect.*
>
> Matthew 5:43-48

Assigned Reading: *The Abba Foundation*, Chapter 6

Chapter Summary

Holiness is wholeness. The Father is not after our behavior but our wholeness. This can be clearly seen in the story where Jesus deals with a woman caught in the act of adultery (John 8:3-11). Somehow, we hold a belief that Jesus loves us unconditionally … until we meet Him. But once we give our lives to Him, things change, and His love becomes conditional. We live under the assumption that once we are His, He loves us based on our performance. We may not acknowledge it, but that's how it often plays out in real life. But the issue is not acceptance, but wholeness.

God doesn't love us any more or any less based on what we do. He is infinite, overflowing, other-centered, unconditional love. He doesn't love us on the basis of our performance; and neither does He stop loving us according to our behavior. Holiness is about being whole—coming to Him and allowing God, the physician of our humanity, to make us whole. In that wholeness, we won't have to continue in our sin. Jesus has come to heal our brokenness, so we don't have to continue in sin any more. This is the Good News! We are no longer subject to sin. We are now free from the law

---

A disciple of Jesus is one who freely receives the Father's love and responds to His presence, evidenced by other-centered love and action.

of sin and death, so we can experience wholeness and eternal life. We have been made alive with Christ, and the Holy Spirit himself comes alongside to help us walk in newness of life. This newness of life involves relational wholeness—a way of being with one another that reflects the way of being of the Father, Son, and Holy Spirit.

Hear the Father saying, "Why would you continue living in the pattern of your old self? Why would you settle for anything less than the fullness of life that I have provided for you? Come, let Me make you whole. I want to bring you to Myself, restore you, make you whole, and then fill you with my Holy Spirit so you can walk in the fullness of holiness." This is what the Father says when He issues the invitation, "Be holy, as I am holy." It's a glorious promise, and a grand invitation.

Questions:

1) Why is it important to understand God's holiness before we can understand His call for us to be holy?

2) How does God's unconditional love inform our understanding of Matthew 5:48: "You therefore must be perfect, as your heavenly Father is perfect."

3) Select a portion of the Gospels where we see Jesus interacting with sinners (e.g. John 8:3-11, Luke 7:39-50 or Matthew 9:10-13, or Mark 2:15-17—but you can choose your own). What was His attitude? Discuss how God's holiness is expressed in Jesus' interaction with sinners. If we are to be holy as He is holy, what should our attitude be toward sinners—those who are broken?

A disciple of Jesus is one who freely receives the Father's love and responds to His presence, evidenced by other-centered love and action.

4) Why is it important for us to know that both *perfect* and *holy* speak of wholeness of being rather than behavior?

5) What do you think about the fact that the Father has made provision for our holiness?

• •

Supplemental Article

Childbirth and the Law

How does the Father and holiness play out when in the books of the Old Testament we see such specific instructions for all the things people must do when they are "unclean"? How does the Hebrew lens help us make sense of such passages? Let me give you one example from Leviticus:

Speak to the people of Israel, saying, If a woman conceives and bears a male child, then she shall be unclean seven days. As at the time of her menstruation, she shall be unclean. And on the eighth day the flesh of his foreskin shall be circumcised. Then she shall continue for thirty-three days in the blood of her purifying. She shall not touch anything holy, nor come into the sanctuary, until the days of her purifying are completed. But if she bears a female child, then she shall be unclean two weeks, as in her menstruation. And she shall continue in the blood of her purifying for sixty-six days. "And when the days of her purifying are completed, whether for a son or for a daughter, she shall bring to the priest at the entrance of the tent of meeting a lamb a year old for a burnt offering, and a pigeon or a turtledove for a sin offering, and he shall offer

A disciple of Jesus is one who freely receives the Father's love and responds to His presence, evidenced by other-centered love and action.

*it before the Lord and make
atonement for her. Then she
shall be clean from the flow
of her blood. This is the law
for her who bears a child,
either male or female. And
if she cannot afford a lamb,
then she shall take two
turtledoves or two pigeons,
one for a burnt offering and
the other for a sin offering.
And the priest shall make
atonement for her, and she
shall be clean.*
Leviticus 12:2-8

A sin offering for giving birth to a baby? This doesn't make sense! And yet, Leviticus 12 is very clear about it. God prescribed laws for the people of Israel—laws having to do with all aspects of their lives. One of those deals with women who give birth. For a son, she is unclean for a week, and then 33 days. For a daughter, she is unclean for two weeks, and then for 66 days. Then, to top it off, she has to offer a burnt offering and a sin offering. Only after that is she declared "clean" again. This notion is hard to understand—that is, of course, under the most common definition of sin.

If we think of "sin" as synonymous with "bad behavior deserving punishment," then God's prescription indicates that the woman must have done something wrong. Having a child is so wrong, in fact, that the punishment is pretty severe! And clearly, with this understanding, having a daughter

is really, really bad. Does this sound like "war on women?"

But what if "sin" is something different? What if these laws show us a totally different aspect of God's heart?

You see, the idea of sin as "missing the mark," rules and punishment is Roman—not Hebrew. For the Hebrew culture, "sin" is the breaking of relationship. And the Law is primarily about preserving the community. It's not judicial but relational.

And what if "unclean" means something different than what we assume from our Western/Roman lens? Let's filter the Leviticus passage about childbearing through the Hebrew relational lens. When a woman gives birth, her body needs time to recover. For nine months she has had significant hormonal alterations—not to mention changes in eating habits, sleep patterns, and endurance in general. How long does it take for her body to be back to "normal?"

Modern medicine recognizes a woman's need for a season of recovery after giving birth to address hormonal changes, swelling, cramping, and even emotional needs. Could it be that our compassionate God knows this and is making room for her to receive the care that she needs?

Perhaps God is saying, "when a woman gives birth, give her room to recover! Don't expect her to be involved in the day-to-day activities of the community. Set her apart until she is done with the

A disciple of Jesus is one who freely receives the Father's love and responds to His presence, evidenced by other-centered love and action.

42

recovery process." (This is hard for us to understand because we are used to living such independent lives; but in that culture, everyone had an active role to play. Think "maternity leave").

Then, at the end of the "recovery" process she is to offer a burnt offering and a sin offering. The burnt offering is a voluntary offering, a "pleasing aroma to the Lord," a sign of total surrender to Him. The sin offering signals to the community that she is ready to be restored to her relational participation in its life. It's not about "appeasing an angry God;" but about celebrating her restoration and receiving her back as a full participant in the community.

• •

Personal Reflection

What is the Lord saying to you?

A disciple of Jesus is one who freely receives the Father's love and responds to His presence, evidenced by other-centered love and action.

A disciple of Jesus is one who freely receives the Father's love and responds to His presence, evidenced by other-centered love and action.

44

Week 7
The Father and Relationships

Meditation Verse

"Love the Lord your God with all your heart and with all your soul and with all your mind." This is the first and greatest commandment. And the second is like it: "Love your neighbor as yourself." All the Law and the Prophets hang on these two commandments. (Matthew 22:37-40)

The verse in context:

> *But when the Pharisees heard that he had silenced the Sadducees, they gathered together. And one of them, a lawyer, asked him a question to test him. "Teacher, which is the great commandment in the Law?" And he said to him, "You shall love the Lord your God with all your heart and with all your soul and with all your mind. This is the great and first commandment. And a second is like it: You shall love your neighbor as yourself. On these two commandments depend all the Law and the Prophets.*
>
> Matthew 22:34-40

Assigned Reading: *The Abba Foundation*, Chapter 7

Chapter Summary

Relationships are important to God—so much so, that He gives us relational guidelines as the way for us to "choose life." The Ten Commandments (or Ten Words) are all relational in nature. They teach us what life looks like when we are relationally whole. *Abba* is inviting us to know Him and trust Him, and paints for us a picture of relational wholeness with one another.

We live in a culture that values individualism, so it's important for us to emphasize God's desire for relationships. When God gives us relational guidelines—with Him and with one another—He does so in order to bring us into a life of holiness where we can fully enjoy His blessing. God is adamant about the need for whole relationships because they reflect His relational way of being. Since we are made in God's image, we are only fulfilled in our personhood in the context of whole and healthy relationships—both with God and with one another.

A disciple of Jesus is one who freely receives the Father's love and responds to His presence, evidenced by other-centered love and action.

All of God's relational guidelines can be summed up in loving one another. Love is the way that the Father, Son, and Holy Spirit are with, for and toward one another, and, by extension, with, for and toward everything they have created. Through Jesus' life we see that love is expressed in manifold ways: Jesus is no respecter of persons; He neither discriminates nor condemns, but breaks through any obstacle looking for ways to bless others—to give in order to make them whole. Jesus finds and affirms value in people, loves unconditionally, and is moved with compassion. He shares others' pain. Jesus doesn't judge, but is quick to forgive and bless to bring about reconciliation. This is the way of holiness: showing love to everyone.

Questions:

1) Discuss the relational aspect of the Ten Commandments. What stands out to you? How does this impact your understanding of God's desire for relationships?

2) Can you identify some areas where you have struggled with God's relational guidelines?

3) What is God saying to you through this chapter about the importance of being "rightly related?"

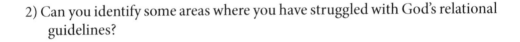

A disciple of Jesus is one who freely receives the Father's love and responds to His presence, evidenced by other-centered love and action.

4) Are there any relationships in your life that need to be restored? Have you been wronged? If so, can you take God at His word, trust Him, and apply what Jesus taught?

5) Think about individualism and how it impacts our relationships. What can you do, in a culture that values individualism, to help others to value relationships?

• •

Supplemental Article

Five Lies That Sabotage Our Time with God

You can trade in the monologue at God for a dialogue with God and increase clarity in hearing His voice. It begins by addressing five lies we believe that sabotage our intimacy with God. Consider these de-energizing beliefs:

1. "Only the super-spiritual hear from God, and I'm certainly not that."

More often than not, we have either bought into the notion that only the "super-spiritual" hear from God, and knowing our own history, can't imagine a thriving spiritual relationship—or perhaps have never seen one. But Gospel of Christ is an invitation for "whosoever will." And really, there

are no "super-spiritual" people; it's only a thought the enemy uses to keep normal people from desiring more of God. God spoke to very ordinary people throughout Scripture.

2. "I'm not sure that God still speaks."

The fact is, all of us hear from God, but we often fail to recognize it for what it is. If you confess Christ, then His Spirit has moved in and He is the One who stirs your heart to connect with God and know the plans of God for you (1 Cor. 2:10-12). Man lives by every word that is continually proceeding from the mouth of God (Matt. 4:4). So, we learn to trust that the Holy Spirit is

A disciple of Jesus is one who freely receives the Father's love and responds to His presence, evidenced by other-centered love and action.

abiding within us, He is guiding us into all truth (1 John 2:20, 27), and it is normal to hear our Heavenly Father speak.

3. "Deep down I'm not sure the pay-off is worth the effort."

This is a tough one, but where many of us live. We have made some efforts in the past to connect to God but were met with frustration of reading a few pages from the Bible and getting sleepy. When we don't see immediate results, our mind tells us that we could be doing other things. We want immediate tangible pay-offs. But immediate gratifications always sabotage long-term investments. Sow to the S/spirit and from the S/spirit you will reap eternal life (Gal 6:8). Keep pen and paper handy; expect to hear His voice daily.

4. "The Bible is the only way to hear from God."

Dr. Jack Hayford says, "God will never say other than what He has said in Scripture, but He will say more." When God speaks to us He rarely speaks in King James English, because that's not how we talk. He speaks to you in ways that you understand best. When you read the Bible, turn it into conversation with God. Say, "Father, I'm asking you to speak to me through your written Word. What do you want to say to me?" But be ready for God to speak in other ways too.

5. "I'm doing OK without it."

No probably not. Jesus said plainly, "Without Me you can do nothing" (John 15:5). We cannot mistake busyness and good efforts for real eternal fruitfulness. And the result only comes through our union with Christ by the Spirit. We've all heard about chopping a tree with a dull ax versus the sharp one; twice the effort, half the result. We are better off to be honest with ourselves to say, "Lord, if You're not in it, I don't want to do it. I need You to speak to me. I want each day to count for eternity."

A disciple of Jesus is one who freely receives the Father's love and responds to His presence, evidenced by other-centered love and action.

Personal Reflection

What is the Lord saying to you?

A disciple of Jesus is one who freely receives the Father's love and responds to His presence, evidenced by other-centered love and action.

49

A disciple of Jesus is one who freely receives the Father's love and responds to His presence, evidenced by other-centered love and action.

50

Week 8
The Father and Freedom

Meditation Verse

So if the Son sets you free, you will be free indeed. (John 8:36)

The verse in context:

So Jesus said to the Jews who had believed him, "If you abide in my word, you are truly my disciples, and you will know the truth, and the truth will set you free." They answered him, "We are offspring of Abraham and have never been enslaved to anyone. How is it that you say, 'You will become free?'"Jesus answered them, "Truly, truly, I say to you, everyone who practices sin is a slave to sin. The slave does not remain in the house forever; the son remains forever. So if the Son sets you free, you will be free indeed. I know that you are offspring of Abraham; yet you seek to kill me because my word finds no place in you. I speak of what I have seen with my Father, and you do what you have heard from your father."

John 8:31-38

Assigned Reading: *The Abba Foundation*, Chapter 8

Chapter Summary

True freedom is not the absence of problems, hindrances, or confinement. It's not the ability to do whatever we want; but on the contrary, the freedom from self-preservation; the freedom from the need to look after our own interests. It's the freedom to be other-centered; the freedom to respond to God without fear or hesitation. It's the freedom to choose life and live in holiness.

The greatest obstacle to this life of freedom is fear, for it leads us to live on the defensive and look out for ourselves. But God reminds us that He is with us and for us, so we have nothing to fear. For us to live in freedom, God has given us His Holy Spirit who mediates the love and presence of God, gives us hope, forms us into the likeness of Jesus, changes our desires, and empowers us to live according to the Father's perfect will. All this by the power of the Spirit. The fruit of the Spirit is the key to relational wholeness; and as such, the key to fullness of life.

Because we are totally loved, totally accepted, secure in God's love—we are free to serve, to love others, to give of ourselves to others. In other words, we are free to be holy, even as He is holy.

A disciple of Jesus is one who freely receives the Father's love and responds to His presence, evidenced by other-centered love and action.

Questions:

1) Contrast the notion of freedom from and freedom to. How is the idea of freedom in Christ different from the ideas of freedom held by those who don't know Christ?

2) Discuss why fear is the greatest inhibitor of other-centered action. Can you think of some examples of this?

3) How does knowing that God is with us and for us help us in living a life of holiness?

4) Of the many things the Holy Spirit does for us, which one stands out to you? Why?

5) Think about the other members of the triad. List the fruit of the Spirit that you see in their lives. Be prepared to share with them how you have been blessed by that fruit.

A disciple of Jesus is one who freely receives the Father's love and responds to His presence, evidenced by other-centered love and action.

Supplemental Article

Daily Meditate on the Word

The Hidden Treasure:

Each week you are meditating on a verse of Scripture so that God imprints its truth on your heart. We rarely hear leaders talk about meditation, but according to the Scripture, those who do not meditate on Scripture will stall in their spiritual growth (John 15:7). There is no zap from an anointed preacher that will fix this. Self-reliance is precisely what must yield in order to meditate at all, though it feels like a loss of control to the Western mind. Through meditation I submit my heart, mind, will, and emotions to God. Those who claim to desire spiritual growth and yet refuse to meditate upon Scripture are deceiving themselves, or have just been poorly trained.

- Biblical Meditation is always accompanied by blessing:

  … you shall meditate in it day and night … then you will make your way prosperous, and then you will have good success.
  Joshua 1:8

  His delight is in the law of the Lord, and in His law he meditates day and night. He shall be like a tree planted by the rivers of water,

that brings forth its fruit in its season, whose leaf also shall not wither; and whatever he does shall prosper.
Psalm 1:1-3

- Meditation on Scripture is the means by which one comes to know by revelation in the heart what was formerly only information in the mind. Memorization is a mental exercise, but meditation is a spiritual exercise where the Holy Spirit breathes the Word to life in a person's spirit:

  My heart was hot within me. While I was musing (meditating) the fire burned; then I spoke with my tongue.
  Psalm 39:3

  Jesus said, "My words, they are spirit and they are life.
  John 6:63

- What one comes to know in the mind can be lost, but what one knows in the S/spirit is eternal and is never lost; revelation (or illumination) transforms at the deepest level of our identity. Martha was busy trying to please and perform; Mary was sitting at Jesus' feet listening, and Jesus said:

A disciple of Jesus is one who freely receives the Father's love and responds to His presence, evidenced by other-centered love and action.

*But one thing is needed,
and Mary has chosen that
good part, which will not be
taken away from her.*
Luke 10:40-42

- Meditation on Scripture involves intently considering the truth of Scripture and repeatedly speaking the words of Scripture: (Hebrew: *Hagah*)—means to mutter, to chew, to speak, to growl; (Joshua 1:8; Psalm 1:1); "to mutter, to say repeatedly (shall not depart from your mouth), to chew."

*A lion that has killed its
prey and is slowly eating
…* (Growling to the other
animals as to say, "It's food, it's
good, and it's mine").
Isaiah 31:4

- Meditation involves remembering, pondering, thinking on the things the Lord has already done (to ponder, remember).

*I will remember the deeds
of the LORD; yes, I will
remember your miracles of
long ago. I will consider all
your works and meditate
on all your mighty deeds.*
Psalm 77:11-12

*I remember the days of
old; I meditate on all Your
works; I muse on the work
of Your hands.*
Psalm 143:5

*Meditate on these things;
give yourself entirely to
them, that your progress
may be evident to all.*
1 Timothy 4:15

- It is by BEHOLDING that we are BECOMING.

*Now the Lord is the Spirit;
and where the Spirit of the
Lord is, there is liberty. But
we all, with unveiled face,
beholding as in a mirror the
glory of the Lord, are being
transformed into the same
image from glory to glory, just
as by the Spirit of the Lord.*
2 Corinthians 3:17-18

The Practice of Biblical Meditation:

- Posture: get your body at rest; sit comfortably, the least motion necessary.
- Minimize distractions: background noise, cell phones …
- Settle on a verse or passage of Scripture.
  - Read that passage or verse out loud several times.
  - Put yourself in the picture or story.
  - Watch the scene unfold— watch God act.
  - Personalize the verse (1st Person), a statement of fact about you.
  - Write the verse down on 3x5 card or easy access in your phone to review many times in the day. Declare

---

*A disciple of Jesus is one who freely receives the Father's love and responds to His
presence, evidenced by other-centered love and action.*

it many times in a day (at red lights, waiting room, office break, etc.)

- "Lord, what do You want to say to me today?"
- "Lord, show me what You want me to see."
- "Lord, what do you want to take off me today?"
- "What truth to replace any lie or misconception?"
- Listen and then write what you hear.

What to Ponder or Mutter:

1. The Greatness of God; His works (Psalm 77:11-12).

- It was David's ability to stay happy.
- How we discover our identity in Christ.

2. Your Future: Imagination, Dreams, and Prophetic Insight

It was the secret of Joseph's survival.

3. The promises of God.

I can do all things through Christ who strengthens me.
Philippians 4:13

May they know that just as I am in You, and You are in Me, they are in us.
John 17:21

• •

Personal Reflection

What is the Lord saying to you?

A disciple of Jesus is one who freely receives the Father's love and responds to His presence, evidenced by other-centered love and action.

A disciple of Jesus is one who freely receives the Father's love and responds to His presence, evidenced by other-centered love and action.

56

Week 9
The Father's Gifts

Meditation Verse

If you, then, though you are evil, know how to give good gifts to your children, how much more will your Father in heaven give good gifts to those who ask him! (Matthew 7:11)

The verse in context:

> *Ask, and it will be given to you; seek, and you will find; knock, and it will be opened to you. For everyone who asks receives, and the one who seeks finds, and to the one who knocks it will be opened. Or which one of you, if his son asks him for bread, will give him a stone? Or if he asks for a fish, will give him a serpent? If you then, who are evil, know how to give good gifts to your children, how much more will your Father who is in heaven give good things to those who ask him!"*
>
> Matthew 7:7-11

Assigned Reading: *The Abba Foundation*, Chapter 9

Chapter Summary

Abba is a giving Father. He reveals Himself as our provider. However, what He provides is not separated from who He is. In the act of creation, God gives of Himself. In the act of redemption God gives of Himself. And in the process of restoration God gives of Himself.

The Holy Spirit is active in the world to fulfill the Father's mission of restoration. He gives gifts that manifest God's love, compassion and power to restore creation back to God's original intent. This is all a work of grace— God's strength at the point of our need (see 2 Cor. 12:9).

By God's grace, we can have peace. By God's grace, we can have joy. By God's grace, we have wisdom both to know and to do His perfect will. By God's grace, we can receive healing. And by God's grace, we can receive everything we need to fulfill our purpose and enjoy fullness of life. How does God distribute His gifts in the earth? He does so through human cooperation. The Father invites us to partner with Him in His mission.

A disciple of Jesus is one who freely receives the Father's love and responds to His presence, evidenced by other-centered love and action.

Questions:

1) Scripture shows how God gives of Himself in the acts of creation, redemption and restoration. Which one strikes you the most? Why?

2) How does understanding God's grace as His strength at the point of our need help you in approaching God confidently in prayer?

3) Of the many ways in which God gives of Himself (peace, joy, wisdom, healing, provision), which one stands out to you? Why?

4) Can you think of some hindrances that keep us from receiving the many gifts that the Father gives? What can we do to overcome them?

5) Make a "gratitude list" of as many things as you can identify that God has freely given you. You may want to include some "*Abba* hugs." Share the list with your group, and explain how making such a list can be helpful in deepening your relationship with God.

A disciple of Jesus is one who freely receives the Father's love and responds to His presence, evidenced by other-centered love and action.

Supplemental Article

The Gifts of the Spirit as God's Compassion

An excerpt from The Gifts of the Spirit for a New Generation[5]

God's nature is love, thus His primary motivation is compassion. But we have misinterpreted God's glory among us through the Orphan mindset of neediness. We feel the need for position, power, possessions and even passions. On every side we see our bankruptcy and need. We are need-minded. We've bought into a needs-driven Gospel and have sought to demonstrate its power through needs-conscious churches and church services that end with needs-driven invitations. We have pastoral leaders that need to prove they can preach moving sermons and demonstrate it by motivating many to come to the altar again. The Orphan spirit is forever coming out of the wilderness but has never quite entered into the Promised Land. Believers are told that they have authority and power in Jesus' name, but every gathering ends in an altar call with a litany of neediness and brokenness expressed. It has become normal to be needy and broken. Thus, the Twentieth and Twenty-First Century Church has interpreted the gifts of the Spirit through the same self-centered lens as the First Century Church (but it's popular to speak about how immature the Corinthians were—which is, in itself, fairly carnal of us).

The saddest part is that God's people get hungry for God to show up in our generation—we rightly get tired of hearing about it only, but never seeing God move. So we are stirred to pray, to seek God, even to fast (that's when you know it's serious!). Then God shows up—He begins to manifest the gifts we long for. But we misinterpret those gifts as something we earned by our seeking God. Our Orphan heart attributes the gifts to ourselves in pride, ownership, and supposed spirituality. Then the stench that it creates drives the next generation to either discount the gifts altogether or to keep them at a comfortable distance. The cycle starts over again.

Of course, the real answer to this cycle of hot and cold is not a new revival but a revelation of the Father's heart in a spirit of Sonship. Sons are comfortable in their place in God and don't see that place as a thing to be grasped (Philippians 2:6). Sons don't have to grasp for something that is already theirs. Sons know where they came from, the authority that is theirs and where they are going—so they can serve others (John 13:1-3). A son can then be other-centered, moved with compassion for others, because he is not concerned with himself.

A disciple of Jesus is one who freely receives the Father's love and responds to His presence, evidenced by other-centered love and action.

Then the Gifts Are Different

The Gifts of the Spirit are not just a special doctrine that some believe and others don't. They are not just the equipment of the super-spiritual to show "special forces" status. The gifts are not a sign that one church has "got it" and the others don't, or one believer has it and others don't. The gifts of the Spirit are but a small part of God's continual overflow of Himself to invade broken creation with His being and bring restoration. The manifestations of the Spirit are the ongoing renewing, healing acts of Jesus by His Spirit, through His Church, to heal all that is broken, to bind up the bruised and set at liberty the captive. It is a pouring out of Himself.

If this is the case, then we don't need to be overly concerned with making a mistake in "being used in the gifts" or "exercising the gifts." The gifts of the Spirit are not a test to see if you can perform. God is looking for any vessel that is willing to be a conduit of His compassion. This is why He uses some very imperfect vessels at times. This is why He uses some people that are "not cool" at times, and even "weird" to many. As one preacher said about delivery pizza, "It's not the box that makes the pizza valuable; it's the pizza that makes the box valuable. God is just looking for an empty, clean box." And even if you make a mistake in the delivery, people still see the compassion of God reaching out to them. You really cannot go wrong as long as you minister with God's heart of compassion to heal, restore and bless—Paul's prescription is "edification, exhortation and comfort."

[5]Kerry Wood, *The Gifts of the Spirit for a New Generation* (Zadok Publishing, 2015).

Personal Reflection

What is the Lord saying to you?

A disciple of Jesus is one who freely receives the Father's love and responds to His presence, evidenced by other-centered love and action.

Week 10
The Father's Call

Meditation Verse

> *If Come to me, all who labor and are heavy laden, and I will give you rest. Take my yoke upon you, and learn from me, for I am gentle and lowly in heart, and you will find rest for your souls. For my yoke is easy, and my burden is light. (Matthew 11:28-30)*

The verse in context:

> *At that time Jesus declared, "I thank you, Father, Lord of heaven and earth, that you have hidden these things from the wise and understanding and revealed them to little children; yes, Father, for such was your gracious will. All things have been handed over to me by my Father, and no one knows the Son except the Father, and no one knows the Father except the Son and anyone to whom the Son chooses to reveal him. Come to me, all who labor and are heavy laden, and I will give you rest. Take my yoke upon you, and learn from me, for I am gentle and lowly in heart, and you will find rest for your souls. For my yoke is easy, and my burden is light."*
>
> Matthew 11:25-30

Assigned Reading: *The Abba Foundation*, Chapter 10

Chapter Summary

Abba's greatest desire is that we be with Him. He made us for relationship and partnership; but the relationship is primary. Abiding with *Abba* is the key to fruitfulness. Abiding with *Abba* gives us power to overcome temptation. Abiding with *Abba* sets us free for a life of service—a life of purpose—as we participate with Him in His mission of restoration. Just as Jesus cultivated His relationship with *Abba* by spending time with Him, so we practice spiritual disciplines as opportunities for encounter. We practice spiritual disciplines to talk to God and hear Him speak to us. Hearing the Father's voice is the catalyst to our freedom and transformation.

We are also called into mission—not as a condition for acceptance, but as a response to His love. The work of the ministry to which *Abba* calls us is always initiated, empowered and guided by the Holy Spirit. It's the overflow

---

A disciple of Jesus is one who freely receives the Father's love and responds to His presence, evidenced by other-centered love and action.

of God's presence, God's love and acceptance that forms us and moves us to share it with others.

Finally, we are called to live in overflow fullness. Living in the fullness of the Spirit is the key to our life in Christ. Living a life of fullness is as simple as (1) accepting the Father's free gift of salvation through Jesus; (2) believing the promise of the Holy Spirit is for you; (3) asking the Father and receiving by faith; and finally, (4) cultivating a life of Spirit-fullness by following Paul's example and instruction. When we allow Him to fill us, participation in His mission is inevitable, and abundant life becomes a reality.

Questions:

1) Why is it important for us to recognize that God's primary call is for us to be *with* Him?

2) Discuss how Jesus was able to overcome temptation. How does that impact the way you can face temptation?

3) Since the purpose of spiritual disciplines is to create opportunities for encounters with *Abba*, discuss the spiritual disciplines that you practice.

4) Which new spiritual disciplines can you use as means to welcome His presence and cultivate a life of spiritual overflow?

A disciple of Jesus is one who freely receives the Father's love and responds to His presence, evidenced by other-centered love and action.

5) Do you have a sense that the Father is calling you into partnership with Him? What might that look like given the way He has formed you and prepared you thus far?

••

Supplemental Article

God's Perfect Will

Can we know God's perfect will? Of course! And it's much simpler than we think. One of the questions people most frequently ask their pastors is, "How can I know God's will for my life?" It is usually asked with an expectation of definitive answers that will guide our decisions as to our career, job, relationships, etc. These are valid questions, and if we talk to the Lord, in prayer, we know that the Holy Spirit will guide us in all our ways (Proverbs 3:5-6).

But God's will for us is much deeper than that. I am convinced that we truly have free will and that God lets us choose many of the details of our lives. At the end of the day, whatever you do, wherever you live, God's will is that you be IN Him, and that you live WITH Him. The rest are just details.

I can say that with certainty because I hear it in Jesus' last prayer, as He addresses His Father and expresses what He desires for His disciples. Here are His words, modified as though He were addressing us directly (rather than praying to the Father). I want you to hear directly what Jesus desires for you:

I have manifested my Father's name to you.

You know that everything the Father gave me is from Him, for I have given you the words that He gave me, and you have received them and have come to know in truth that I came from the Father; and you have believed that the Father sent me.

I have asked my Father to keep you in His name, which my Father gave me, that you may be one, even as my Father and I are one.

I want for you to have my joy fulfilled in you. I have given you my Father's word, and the

A disciple of Jesus is one who freely receives the Father's love and responds to His presence, evidenced by other-centered love and action.

world has hated you because you are not of the world, just as I am not of the world.

I don't want you to be taken out of the world, but that my Father will keep you from the evil one.

You are not of the world, just as I am not of the world.

I want for you to be sanctified in the truth; my Father's word is truth.

As my Father sent me into the world, so I have sent you into the world.

For your sake I consecrated myself, that you also may be sanctified in truth.

I ask my Father for those who will believe in me through your word, that you may all be one.

Just as my Father is in me, and I am in my Father, my desire is that you also may be in us, so that the world may believe that my Father has sent me.

I have given to you the glory that my Father gave, **that you may be one** *even as we are one: I in my Father, and my Father in me.*

My desire is that you may become perfectly one, so that the world may know that my Father sent me and loved you just as my Father loved me.

I desire that you also may be with me where I am.

I want you to see my glory *that my Father gave me because my Father loved me before the foundation of the world.*

You know that my Father sent me. I made His name known to you, and I will continue to make it known, ***that the love with which my Father has loved me may be in you, and I in you.***
John 17:6-26

Live your life in relationship with God. Receive the perfect love of the Father, so you can enjoy being one with Him, according to His will. Walk with him. Open your heart to Him. Let Him change your "want tos"—and you will live in His perfect will.

A disciple of Jesus is one who freely receives the Father's love and responds to His presence, evidenced by other-centered love and action.

Personal Reflection

What is the Lord saying to you?

*A disciple of Jesus is one who freely receives the Father's love and responds to His
presence, evidenced by other-centered love and action.*

65

A disciple of Jesus is one who freely receives the Father's love and responds to His presence, evidenced by other-centered love and action.

66

Congratulations!

You have completed

The Abba FOUNDATION

Here's your invitation to **take the next step** in *The Abba Journey* toward living as a son/daughter who has nothing to hide, nothing to prove, nothing to fear, and nothing to lose.

The Abba Factor, the second part of this trilogy, will allow you to see yourself through the Father's eyes. You will see that the real war is between two mindsets—the orphan spirit and the spirit of sonship. You will see clearly that the whole world has been plunged into this orphan heart. The contrast between the progression of the orphan spirit and the progression of sonship will be so obvious that you will know exactly where you are and how the Lord is working to establish a sonship mentality in you. Finally, you will understand that sonship is not a place to get to, but a way of knowing and seeing yourself through the eyes of *Abba*.

Part 2: *The Abba Factor: Seeing Yourself Through the Eyes of the Father*, by Kerry Wood. Burkhart Books, 2018. ISBN: 978-1-940359-61-8

Part 3: *The Abba Formation: The Holy Spirit's Role in Your Personal Transformation*, by Kerry Wood. Burkhart Books, 2018. ISBN: 978-1-940359656.

Also, remember that Jesus told us to "go into all the world and make disciples of all nations" (Matthew 28:19). **Consider inviting two other friends to join you on *The Abba Journey***. Form a triad and lead them through the journey.

Let's fulfill the Great Commission together!

The *Abba* FACTOR

Sonship is not received by information, education, or even inspiration, by the revelation of the Holy Spirit.

Week 1
Invitation to the Joy Ride

Meditation Verse

I will not leave you [as] orphans; I will come to you. (John 14:18)

The verse in context:

1And I will ask the Father, and he will give you another advocate to help you and be with you forever—the Spirit of truth. The world cannot accept him, because it neither sees him nor knows him. But you know him, for he lives with you and will be in you. I will not leave you as orphans; I will come to you.

John 14:16-18

Assigned Reading: *The Abba Factor*, Introduction and Chapter 1

Chapter Summary

There are many ways the enemy wants to put us in bondage—and he uses traumatic experiences in life, misinterpreting those events with subtle lies about God and us—to convince us that we are orphans, abandoned by God. But the Holy Spirit is not a travel agent but a tour guide—He is in us now, walking with us every step of our path toward total restoration as sons and daughters.

The first fundamental reality of sonship is to understand that God is a revealer. He has nothing to hide. He's giving Himself away completely to make Himself known. The second fundamental reality is that what you believe is the lens through which you see and interpret everything that ever happens to you. Whether you knew it or not, you have had an interpreter throughout your life (either Satan or Holy Spirit) interpreting every event you've ever had through the filter of your believing.

Man cannot be transformed by information alone; if information alone could transform, we would have been set free a long time ago, and those with the highest IQ would naturally be the most free. But the Good News comes to our spirits, not our minds, to be received by simple faith, not by intellect.

Sonship is not received by information, education, or even inspiration, but by the revelation of the Holy Spirit

Questions:

1) In the Introduction the author introduces the significance of Jesus' use of the Aramaic term "*Abba*" when referring to God the Father. Why is this significant for our understanding (p. 13)?

2) What are some examples that confirm to us that God's nature is to reveal Himself, to make Himself known, rather than to conceal Himself?

3) How does Satan use traumatic experiences as "entry points" to build strongholds in our lives? Can you think of an example in your own life where fear, failure, or the need to prove was born out of a traumatic experience?

4) In the supplemental reading, what experiences in Steve Job's childhood might have been traumatic "entry points" the enemy could have used?

5) What are some examples of how the Holy Spirit brings us into experiences with God that set us free from past bondage?

Sonship is not received by information, education, or even inspiration,
but by the revelation of the Holy Spirit

6) When you read about the red mustang convertible (the "Joy Ride"), have you considered what seat you might be sitting in? Can you explain?

• •

Supplemental Article

Steve Jobs: The Orphan Drive

Steve Jobs, billionaire entrepreneur and Apple co-founder, was given up for adoption at birth. His biological parents were unmarried college students at a time when abortion was illegal in the U.S. His biological mother, Joanne Schieble, left the University of Wisconsin and went to San Francisco to give birth, where Steve was adopted by his new parents, Paul and Clara Jobs.

His biological father, Abdulfattah Jandali, was a Syrian Muslim immigrant who later married Ms Schieble. He has said they did not want to put their baby up for adoption, but his girlfriend's parents would not initially allow her to marry an Arab man. Under pressure from her parents and fearing scandal, Ms Schieble traveled to San Francisco to have the baby. Steven Paul, as his adoptive parents named him, was born on February 24, 1955.[6]

His adoptive parents were Armenian and unable to have children. Steve was later joined in the family by his adopted sister Patti Jobs, born in 1958. Steve was one of those nerdy kids at school that was bullied to the point that his parents moved the family to Los Altos (Silicon Valley).

When Steve eventually discovered who his biological parents were, he made contact with his mother and his biological sister, with whom he later became close friends. But according to his biological father, Steve never made contact with him, even up to Steve's death.

Adopted children sometimes wrestle with feelings of abandonment and self-worth, wondering why their parents might have given them up for adoption.

[6]https://www.telegraph.co.uk/technology/steve-jobs/8811345/Steve-Jobs-adopted-child-who-never-met-his-biological-father.html

Sonship is not received by information, education, or even inspiration, but by the revelation of the Holy Spirit

Like many children who have been abandoned, Jobs would repeat the pattern as an adult. When he learned, in his twenties, that a live-in girlfriend was pregnant, he questioned whether he was the father. And despite a sense of gratitude that his own life had been spared in the womb, he considered an abortion as a solution to the pregnancy. Once his daughter, Lisa, was born, he refused to acknowledge her as his own for several years, but finally agreed to a paternity test and then began to pay child support.

Decades later, Lisa's mother told Isaacson that "being put up for adoption left Jobs full of broken glass."[7]

In many cases, this sense of worthlessness can drive the orphan heart to prove worth in other ways. Steve Jobs' own personal drive was legendary.

A co-worker at Apple made a similar observation: "The key question about Steve is why he can't control himself at times from being so reflexively cruel and harmful to some people.

"That goes back to being abandoned at birth. The real underlying problem was the theme of abandonment in Steve's life."[8]

But the truth is, his life was worth more than he could have imagined even before he started his famous computer company in his garage. His Father in heaven had placed a value on him before anyone but God Himself even knew he was alive.

Although God wants you to make the most of your life here on earth, and to use the gifts and abilities that He's given, one need not be driven to prove self-worth to Him or others; only He sets our true value. The Spirit of sonship is a conviction an awareness (created in the depths of one's being by the Holy Spirit), that one's natural ancestry is trumped by the spiritual reality of the Father's claims upon our life, with all the rights and privileges that come with it.

[7]http://www.ncregister.com/daily-news/steve-jobs-an-unwanted-child
[8]Walter Isaacson, *Steve Jobs*. New York: Simon and Schuster, 2011.

Sonship is not received by information, education, or even inspiration, but by the revelation of the Holy Spirit

Personal Reflection

What is the Lord saying to you?

Week 2
The Orphan Spirit on International Scale

Meditation Verse

> *In love He predestined us for adoption to sonship through Jesus Christ, in accordance with His pleasure and will. (Eph. 1:5)*

The verse in context:

> *For he chose us in him before the creation of the world to be holy and blameless in his sight. In love he predestined us for adoption to sonship through Jesus Christ, in accordance with his pleasure and will—to the praise of his glorious grace, which he has freely given us in the One he loves. In him we have redemption through his blood, the forgiveness of sins, in accordance with the riches of God's grace.*
>
> Ephesians 1:4-7, NIV

Assigned Reading: *The Abba Factor*, Chapter 2

Chapter Summary

When Adam sinned, he (and the human family) alienated himself from the life of God. That alienation produced an orphan spirit that is visible on a global scale. The conflict of the Middle East is most easily understood as an ongoing war between sons and orphans—those that have a homeland (inheritance) and those who do not. We can see that the orphan spirit is not just about what bad people do, but is at work in all of us, even the great patriarchs of the Scripture.

This orphan heart is rooted in our father-relationships—the desire to prove that we deserve our father's approval, or an attempt to show his disapproval was wrong. People in both high and low places are driven by an orphan mindset. Satan uses the imperfections of those that God has put in authority in our lives as entry points for an orphan spirit—and none of us get perfect parents.

We live in a orphaned world, but in the Father's love we were predestined for adoption to sonship through Jesus Christ, before the foundation of the world (Eph. 1:4-7).

Sonship is not received by information, education, or even inspiration, but by the revelation of the Holy Spirit

Questions:

1. The author raises the possibility that some cultures show more resilience and stability than others (p. 30). Do you see evidence for this, and what might be the common causes for such differences?

2. Think about the possible connection between atheism and the orphan spirit (p. 30-31). How might a refusal to believe in God contribute to a sense of orphan heart or abandonment?

3. What are some examples of "great men" of the Bible who had signs of an orphan spirit (p. 32-34)?

4. What is the connection between lacking a healthy father-relationship and driven-ness to prove something? Can you think of examples of "successful people" with poor or non-existent relationships with their father?

5. How can someone with an orphan spirit and someone living in sonship both look successful?

Sonship is not received by information, education, or even inspiration,
but by the revelation of the Holy Spirit

Part 2
THE *ABBA* JOURNEY The *Abba* FACTOR

6. What stands out to you from Absalom's story that seems significant to the development of an orphan heart?

7. Have you ever been tempted to criticize or challenge someone in authority because you felt they weren't capable or you could do better? Why is that foreign to a sons' way of thinking?

• •

Supplemental Article

Orphans Without A Home

We understand that, in Christ Jesus, there is neither Jew nor Greek ... that Jesus has paid the same price to redeem every man and woman on the planet. This adaption of the brief history of the quest for a Palestinian State is by no means meant to imply that Jesus doesn't love Palestinian peoples, no matter the nationality, as any other person—He has redeemed every nation, tongue and people. But the history is to highlight a global conflict between *the spirit of sonship and the orphan* spirit that has existed since the time of Abraham.

After World War I, Palestine was within the British sphere, and in 1917 the British, through Foreign Minister Lord Balfour, issued a declaration calling for

the establishment of a Jewish homeland in Palestine. The Balfour Declaration did not call for the creation of an independent Palestinian state, but in 1921 some 80% of the territory designated for the British Mandate of Palestine was carved out to create Transjordan (Jordan)–thereby excluding such lands from the plan for a Jewish state. Today, Palestinians comprise more than half of Jordan's population.

The remaining 20% of the British Mandate was further divided by the UN, in its 1947 Partition Plan: part for a Jewish state, and part for a Palestinian Arab state. The opportunity for a peaceful "two state solution" was at hand. The Jews accepted the UN

Sonship is not received by information, education, or even inspiration,
but by the revelation of the Holy Spirit

79

Partition Plan. The Palestinians did not. Palestinians can only blame their own leaders for rejecting the UN Plan. And, many Palestinian Arabs joined forces with Egypt, Syria, Iraq and Lebanon in a war to eradicate Israel in 1948. Many on both sides lost their lives, and the war created an enormous refugee problem, but it did nothing to advance the cause of a Palestinian state.

Israel prevailed in the 1948 war, but for the next 19 years Jordan occupied the West Bank–the region now proposed as the heart of a Palestinian state, just as the UN had proposed in 1947. One might ask why Jordan did not establish a Palestinian state in the West Bank. One might wonder why none of the Arab states, rich with oil and lands, do not establish a territory for the Palestinians. Whatever the answer may be, the blame does not lie with Israel.

The status of the West Bank changed in 1967. Israel, again facing a war of extermination by its Arab neighbors, not only prevailed but pushed back its would-be conquerors, thereby taking control of the "occupied" territories. The UN called for "land for peace" in Resolution 242. Israel, having taken possession of new territories in a war it did not seek, now at least had tangible bargaining power.

In 1979 Israel returned the Sinai Peninsula to Egypt in a historic "land for peace" deal. The resulting peace treaty, which still holds today, proved that "land for peace" can work when there are true partners in peace. Egypt's Anwar Sadat was indeed such a partner. He was a courageous visionary willing to take bold steps to break the cycle of violence that has long plagued Arab-Israeli relations. Yet the reaction of his Arab neighbors revealed a spirit at work against Israel. Sadat was branded a traitor by his Arab brothers, and Egypt became a reviled outcast. The Arab League suspended Egypt and imposed economic sanctions against it. Egypt was ousted from the Organization of Arab Petroleum Exporting Countries. Within two years, Sadat was assassinated by members of the Egyptian Islamic Jihad.

Powerful Palestinian factions are set against peace with Israel. Significant progress was made in Oslo in 1993; the PLO agreed to renounce terrorism and to recognize Israel's right to exist in peace. But Hamas–a Palestinian offshoot of the Muslim Brotherhood–responded to Oslo with harsh opposition and ramped up suicide bombings in Israel. And in 2000, another opportunity for Palestinian statehood was squandered. About 95% of the West Bank was offered to the Palestinians in the Camp David peace talks (along with additional territory within pre-1967 Israel), with parts of East Jerusalem to serve as the capital of a Palestinian State, and Gaza was included as well, but that offer was rejected by the Palestinians.

Sonship is not received by information, education, or even inspiration,
but by the revelation of the Holy Spirit

Some important questions must be asked: 1) What would have happened had the Palestinians accepted the UN Partition in 1947? 2) What would have happened had the Palestinians accepted the proposal for statehood at Camp David in 2000? 3) Why did the Palestinian leadership reject these opportunities? 4) What is it about the orphan spirit that wants what the son has, but will not settle for peace?

History has shown that the "problem" with these offers was that Palestinian leaders would have had to finally accept the existence of the Jewish state (i.e. acknowledge sonship). Many moderate Palestinians have long been prepared to accept this, and enjoy the benefits of peace. But extremists such as Hamas would rather die than coexist with Israel. Their founding charter plainly explains this. Bombing buses and restaurants, launching thousands of rockets into civilian populations, building terror tunnels instead of schools or hospitals is the manifestation of an insanity that

would rather commit suicide than coexist in peace. The ongoing war between the orphan spirit and sonship is not new. It is the orphan spirit on a global scale. But God has already set His plan in motion:

*"For he chose us in him [Jesus Christ] before the creation of the world to be holy and blameless in his sight. In love **he predestined us for adoption to sonship through Jesus Christ**, in accordance with his pleasure and will ..."*
Eph. 1:4-5

God's plan is global, but not national. It is a personal plan to redeem us one by one into right relationship to Himself through personal faith in Jesus Christ.

Adapted by Dr. Kerry Wood from John C. Landa's article entitled "Why There is No Palestinian State: Here Are Some Reasons." http://blogs.timesofisrael.com/why-is-there-no-palestinian-state/ Dec. 29, 2014.

Sonship is not received by information, education, or even inspiration, but by the revelation of the Holy Spirit

Personal Reflection

What is the Lord saying to you?

Week 3

The Father's Invitation to Sonship

Meditation Verse

God's Spirit touches our spirits and confirms who we really are. We know who he is, and we know who we are: Father and children. (Romans 8:15, The Message)

The verse in context:

This resurrection life you received from God is not a timid, grave-tending life. It's adventurously expectant, greeting God with a childlike "What's next, Papa?" God's Spirit touches our spirits and confirms who we really are. We know who he is, and we know who we are: Father and children. And we know we are going to get what's coming to us— an unbelievable inheritance!

Romans 8:15-16 The Message

Assigned Reading: *The Abba Factor*, Chapter 3

Chapter Summary

There are really only two spirits (spiritual mindsets) at war in the world today; the orphan spirit and the spirit of sonship. God sent a personal invitation to the orphan world by sending His own Son, to show us what the Father is really like, and to know that a way has been prepared for all to return to Father's house.

The significance of Romans 8:14-17 is that Paul articulates clearly and succinctly that sons know who their father is, they know they have a home, and know they have an inheritance as joint heirs with our elder brother, Jesus Christ. Orphan thinking promotes a tendency to focus on the negative, the faults and failures of our flawed natural parents and leaders.

Even the First Century Jewish believers in Messiah had struggled with an orphan spirit and were tempted to go back to the Law of Moses: Jesus plus something else. In Jesus' story of The Father's Heart (The Prodigal Son story), we discover that one son was defiant and the other compliant, but both lived as orphan-thinking—wanting the father's "stuff" more than enjoying intimacy with the father.

Sonship is not received by information, education, or even inspiration, but by the revelation of the Holy Spirit

Questions:

1) What are the two spirits (spiritual mindsets) that are at war in the world today for the hearts of mankind?

2) According to Romans 8:14-17, what are the three primary things a believer knows that he/she possesses as a son?

3) What difference do you think an inward awareness of this "knowing" (Romans 8:14-17) would have on a person in practical ways?

4) In the "Prodigal Son Story" (Luke 15), which of the two sons were motivated by an orphan spirit (orphan thinking)? What are the tale-tell signs?

5) The primary purpose of all of Jesus' parables was to re-frame what people thought about God and His kingdom. Jesus' primary purpose of the Prodigal Story was not about the sons, but about what The Father is really like. What does this story reveal about the nature of God? And why did Jesus need to go to such lengths to communicate the Father's heart?

Sonship is not received by information, education, or even inspiration, but by the revelation of the Holy Spirit

Supplemental Article

The Orphan Spirit Bargains; Sons Listen

Have you ever bargained with God? The orphan spirit works corporately, because it works personally, and bargaining is a certain indicator. Here's an example; first Israel, and then Jephthah whom Israel chooses (in its own image) as leader. It would be best if you would read Judges, chapter 10 and 11, first. In Judges 10 and 11, we come upon another painful drama of Israel's wayward heart which leads them to idol worship, subsequent crisis, and deal-making.

The tribes of Israel are facing a war with the Ammonites but have no moral compass—they have been worshipping all the gods of the surrounding foreigners (11:6) and have no real relationship with God or confidence in Him, so rather than seek the Lord for His direction, they only ask for deliverance, and as most of us have done at one time or another, we repent ... with a bargain, *"We have sinned. Do with us whatever You think is best, but please rescue us now. Then they got rid of their foreign gods ..."* (11:15).

Notice carefully, that though Israel had just "repented", they still acted as orphans. Rather than seek the Lord for His voice, they assembled together to seek out the most courageous man among them. They say, *"Whoever will launch the attack against that Ammonites will be the leader of all Israel"* (Judges 10:18). They are willing to bargain, to make a deal. That makes perfect human sense, right? But they don't even realize that they are leaning on the arm of human strength and capability as their source of deliverance.

Chapter 11 opens with the background of Jephthah and introduces him as "a mighty warrior." But he wears the typical garb of the orphan spirit. His father is Gilead and his mother was a prostitute. But Gilead's actual wife "bore him sons, and when they were grown up, they drove Jephthah away" (11:2). Do you see the picture? He is raised in rejection, a bastard son, slandered by the "real brothers," and eventually (when it was time to step into inheritance) his brother drove him out of the house. His sonship is challenged. His inheritance is denied. He is driven from his home and from his father. And how does someone live with such rejection? He compensates by becoming a "mighty warrior" (Judges 11:1-3).

Facing imposing Ammonite armies, and compromised due to their own idol worship, those who had driven Jephthah away call him back to lead them, not on the basis of relationship, but because he could perform—he's a mighty warrior. They said, *"Be our*

---

*Sonship is not received by information, education, or even inspiration,
but by the revelation of the Holy Spirit*

commander, so we can fight the Ammonites" (11:5-6).

Jephthah becomes a leader of Israel, not because he knows God and has learned to depend upon God via communion and relationship, but because he has learned to fight (the game of human power). From a human perspective it seems Jephthah's strategy worked. He's elected as their leader. Prove that you are better than they said by becoming the best in your field. Prove the world wrong.

The problem is, the orphan spirit doesn't leave just because a person is promoted into leadership. In fact, the new pressures of leadership will only bring the insecurities and bargaining to the surface. This becomes clear when Jephthah, facing the greatest challenge of his life, cannot actually trust his own warfare abilities, and makes a vow to the Lord. He says to the Lord, *"If You will indeed deliver the people of Ammon into my hands, then it will be that whatever comes out of the doors of my house to meet me, when I return in peace from the people of Ammon, shall surely be the Lord's, and I will offer it up as a burnt offering."*

You can read the sad account (11:34-39) of Jephthah, arriving home after the victory, to have his only child come out of the door of his house. His bargaining cost him dearly.

We read that story and immediately question God. Why would God want Jephthah to offer his own daughter in sacrifice? Is He that kind of angry, vengeful god? No. The reality is, God graciously gave the armies of Ammon into Israel's hands because they repented. But neither Israel nor Jephthah sought the Lord before entering that battle. There is no indication that God put Jephthah up to that bargain, though we can admire Jephthah for keeping his vow.

When we don't know God as *Abba*, an infinitely-loving father who only wants good for His children, we will approach Him as a boss, merchant, or corruptible judge who is looking to make a deal. If we don't know God as a father who accepts us as we are, in whatever condition we were born, we will try to "power up" to prove our identity.

You see, it's really all about your identity—knowing and living in the revelation of your sonship through Jesus Christ by the Holy Spirit. Without a revelation of your sonship, you cannot simply change your mind, think new thoughts, and decide to walk as a son. All the "change your thinking" training does no good without a spirit of wisdom and revelation—the Holy Spirit convicting you in your spirit that you are a son/daughter of God. You may even learn the "sonship language" and be able to use the words of sonship and the orphan spirit, but if you haven't been transformed by the Holy Spirit in your spirit, you will revert to orphan thinking and behavior when the pressure is on.

Sonship is not received by information, education, or even inspiration, but by the revelation of the Holy Spirit

What kind of supernatural victory would Jephthah and Israel have seen if they had sought the Lord and listened to His voice, rather than making bargains with God? How often do we bargain with God—"God, if you'll just do this for me, just this time, I'll never do so-and-so again … I'll serve you the rest of my life … quit that addiction …?" What kind of "birth mark" do you carry that seems to drive you to either victimization or hyper-victory? How would life be different if you simply lived in the revelation that you are a son— having nothing to hide, nothing to prove, nothing to fear, and nothing to lose? What would life look like if you didn't have to keep up with the Joneses because the Father knows what His sons and daughters need even before you ask, much less bargain or make a vow?

Daniel, among others, would be a great contrast in narrative. He knows who he is, stays in communion with God, listens, and when the pressure is on, he trusts himself to God, who preserves him supernaturally in the lions' den. Could it be that we don't see more miraculous interventions because we are bargaining instead of resting in a revelation and listening?

• •

Personal Reflection

What is the Lord saying to you?

Sonship is not received by information, education, or even inspiration,
but by the revelation of the Holy Spirit

Week 4
The Fathering Spirit Has Come

Meditation Verse

> *And he will turn the hearts of the fathers to the children, And the hearts of the children to their fathers. (Malachi 4:6)*

The verse in context:

> *Behold, I will send you Elijah the prophet Before the coming of the great and dreadful day of the Lord. And he will turn the hearts of the fathers to the children, And the hearts of the children to their fathers, Lest I come and strike the earth with a curse."*
>
> Malachi 4:4-6

Assigned Reading: *The Abba Factor*, Chapter 4

Chapter Summary

We often miss the main thing that God has for us because we settle for secondary things; He sends His Son but we settle for memorizing some Scriptures. He puts His Spirit within us but we settle for a weekend worship experience. In short, we exchange the Person of Jesus for principles and precepts. The orphan spirit will take those things freely given by God and turn them into measurements to self-promote or bolster self-esteem. Another way to say this is that when we fail to realize we are one with the Head, who is Christ, we will settle for good performance, personal legacy, or best practices rather than an eternity-shaping movement to recover the orphan planet.

The Old Testament ended with the curse of the orphan spirit upon the earth, but the New Testament era opened with the Fathering Spirit being released in the ministry of Jesus by the Holy Spirit. Jesus came as partner with the Holy Spirit to show us what happens when sons know who they are and how to simply live in the Father's love and presence.

Sonship is not received by information, education, or even inspiration, but by the revelation of the Holy Spirit

Questions:

1) What is the significance of the closing of the Old Testament and the opening of the New Testament with reference to "the spirit of Elijah?"

2) Which of the "You might still think like an orphan if ..." statements spoke to you the most?

3) Rabbinical teaching has asserted that "the highest form of worship is the study of Scripture." But why does the orphan mindset tend to replace the worship of the Person of Jesus with principles and precepts (see John 5:39-40)?

4) Who is the "fathering spirit" that Jesus reveals in John, Chapter 14 (see pages 56-57)?

5.) In practical terms, how would our lives be different if our hearts were so turned to The Father that our highest priority would be to finish His unfinished business?

Supplemental Article

The Promise of the Father

From Old to New Testament

*Behold, I send the Promise
of My Father upon you; but
tarry in the city of Jerusalem
until you are endued with
power from on high.*

We have been allowed to see the activity of The Holy Spirit from the creation of the universe and throughout the Old Testament. The Bible describes various activities of the Holy Spirit during Old Testament times and yet His ministry did not become prominent among God's people until Jesus began to minister. Luke tells us that what Jesus did, He did by the power of the Holy Spirit:

*How God anointed Jesus
of Nazareth with the Holy
Spirit and with power, who
went about doing good
and healing all that were
oppressed of the devil, for
God was with Him.*

Acts 10:38

But this was markedly different from the Old Testament. The spirit of God came upon individuals in the Old Testament to equip them for special acts of power, service, or words. But the primary work of the Holy Spirit in the Old Testament was to lead people to an awareness that righteous living in God was possible—but not without the indwelling Spirit.

Note that in the Old Testament times the Holy Spirit came upon or "filled" only a few people, but it was a temporary empowerment. There was no general outpouring of the Holy Spirit on all Israel (Joel 2: 28-29; Acts 2:4, 16-18); the outpouring of the Spirit in this larger sense did not begin until the great day of Pentecost was fulfilled after Jesus had ascended up to the Father, and the Father, by Jesus (as Head of the Church) fulfilled the long-awaited promise and poured out the Spirit globally ("on all flesh").

The Father's Promise is Full Power, Partnership, and Sonship on Messiah

The Old Testament looks forward to the coming age of the Spirit, first in the life and ministry of Messiah, then in the Church. On several occasions the prophets prophesied about the role that the Spirit would play in the life of the coming Messiah. Isaiah especially characterized the coming king and servant of the Lord as one on whom the Spirit of God would rest in a special way (Isaiah 11:1-2; 42:1; 61:1-3). The chief characteristic of Messiah would be an empowering partnership with the Spirit:

*Sonship is not received by information, education, or even inspiration,
but by the revelation of the Holy Spirit*

*There shall come forth a
Rod from the stem of Jesse,
And a Branch shall grow
out of his roots. **The Spirit
of the <u>Lord</u> shall rest upon
Him**, The Spirit of <u>wisdom</u>
and <u>understanding</u>,
The Spirit of <u>counsel</u>
and <u>might</u>, The Spirit of
<u>knowledge</u> and of the <u>fear</u>
of the Lord.*
Isa. 11:1-2

*Behold! My Servant whom
I uphold, My Chosen One
in whom My soul delights!
**I have put My Spirit
upon Him** ....*
Isa. 42:1-2

***The Spirit of the Lord
God is upon Me***, *Because
the Lord has anointed
Me To preach ... to heal
... to proclaim ... to open
prison doors ....*
Isa. 61:1-3

When Jesus read the words from Isaiah chapter 61 in his hometown synagogue at Nazareth, he ended with, *"Today this Scripture is fulfilled in your hearing"* (Luke 4:21). This is the Spirit resting upon Messiah to reveal the heart of the misunderstood Father.

The Father's Promise is Full Power, Partnership, and Sonship on Believers

Secondly, other Old Testament prophecies looked forward to the time when there would be an outpouring, not just on the Messiah, but general Spirit-outpouring on all of God's people. One of the most prominent of these passages is Joel 2:28-29, a passage that Peter quoted in his sermon on the day of Pentecost (Acts 2:17-18). But a greater significance and purpose can be found in Isaiah 32:15-17; 44:3-5; 59:20-21; Ezekiel 11:19-20; Ezekiel 36:26-27; 37:14; and 39:29. For example, watch the breakthrough significance of the Father's Promise upon believers:

*For I will take you <u>from
among the nations</u>, gather
you out of all countries,
and bring you into your
own land. Then I will
<u>sprinkle clean water on you</u>,
and you shall be clean; I will
cleanse you from all your
filthiness and from all your
idols. I will <u>give you a new
heart</u> and <u>put a new spirit
within you</u>; I will take the
heart of stone out of your
flesh and give you a heart of
flesh. **I will put My Spirit
within you** and <u>cause you
to walk</u> in My statutes, and
you will keep My judgments
and do them.*
Ezek. 36:24-27

The is Promise of the Father is clearly more than a ticket to Heaven. The Father's Promise, in essence, pointed to an anticipated day when the life and power of His Spirit would come upon His people. They would become a New Creation. They would have a new nature. They would be enabled to prophesy, see visions, have prophetic dreams, live lives of obedience and power. And He would <u>cause them</u> to live lives of holiness, not by the force-of-will to keep the law, but by an internally empowered rightness that would pour forth by the indwelling Holy Spirit.

In short, The Promise of the Father, is the promise of sons and daughters restored to the Father, and the Father restored to sons and daughters ... not just in a legal provision for sins forgiven and a promise of a home in heaven, but the full partnership of sons, here and now, who are on the Father's mission, to bring many sons to glory (Heb. 2:10).

• •

Personal Reflection

What is the Lord saying to you?

Sonship is not received by information, education, or even inspiration,
but by the revelation of the Holy Spirit

Week 5

The Progression to an Orphan Spirit

Meditation Verse

> *But each one is tempted when he is drawn away by his own desires and enticed. Then, when desire has conceived, it gives birth to sin; and sin, when it is full-grown, brings forth death. (James 1:14-15)*

The verse in context:

> *Blessed is the man who endures temptation; for when he has been approved, he will receive the crown of life which the Lord has promised to those who love Him. Let no one say when he is tempted, "I am tempted by God"; for God cannot be tempted by evil, nor does He Himself tempt anyone. But each one is tempted when he is drawn away by his own desires and enticed. Then, when desire has conceived, it gives birth to sin; and sin, when it is full-grown, brings forth death.*
>
> James 1:12-15

Assigned Reading: *The Abba Factor*, Chapter 5

Chapter Summary

Inroads are opened for the orphan spirit very early in our lives when mistakes, especially from our parents, are received as rejection. We believe a lie that we are not loved or not worth being loved. We lose faith to let others meet our needs, learn to keep people at a safe distance, and feel that we have to achieve by ourselves.

At the same time we can begin to feel "everyone owes me something." The orphan spirit seeks to control, manipulate and take from anyone who demonstrates sonship—that is, anyone who walks in a sense of ownership or authority becomes the target of the orphan spirit; the orphan spirit tries to get a hold of something that the son has, rationalizing that "the son didn't do anything to deserve what he has."

The orphan spirit traffics in anxiety, guilt and a sense of homelessness. "Homelessness" becomes a state of mind and heart that whispers, "I don't fit in, I don't have a place, I'm too different." Or it goes on the offensive to grasp for someone else's place. In short, failed expectations begin at a very early age and can set us up for a sense of personal rejection. We lose trust in

Sonship is not received by information, education, or even inspiration, but by the revelation of the Holy Spirit

95

others, develop a fear of lack, then self-protect. The self-protection nurtures an independent spirit which teaches us to control our relationships.

Questions:

1) Can you think of a situation or event in your own childhood, or in the life of one of your children, where a parent's unintentional act, forgetfulness, or outright mistake was received or interpreted as personal rejection?

2) What does Sigmund Freud's story tell you about how misplaced expectations can open the door to strongholds?

3) What does Lee Harvey Oswald's story tell you about Satan's strategy to isolate us from others with an independent, self-reliant spirit?

4) If Satan's mode of operation is to reinterpret the events of your life into failed expectations, personal rejection, and loss of trust, what might that tell us about the Holy Spirit's role (See John 14:16-17)?

5) When you think of your own parents, what kind of emotions surface? Is there anything lingering in your own heart and soul between you and your parents (or your children) that need help? Can you ask your triad or small group to pray with you about this right now?

• •

Supplemental Article

Contrasting Impacts on the Orphan Spirit and Sonship

Adam and Eve alienated themselves from God the Father through disobedience. Since that day an orphan spirit has permeated the earth causing untold damage. Almost immediately after the fall in Eden, the fruit of this orphan spirit resulted in jealousy, culminating in Cain murdering his brother Abel because God the Father didn't receive Cain's offering. In contemporary society, large amounts of people are not only alienated from God but are brought up without the loving care of a nuclear family and/or security of their biological fathers.

The emotional, physical and spiritual ills of society can be traced to human alienation from God and the subsequent alienation from biological fathers (and mothers). Orphan-hearted men have a hard time connecting spiritually and emotionally with their spouses, their children, those in spiritual and vocational authority. At the

root, they have difficulty accepting and loving themselves. There are presently millions of incarcerated men who have acted out of violence and rebellion because their earthly fathers abandoned them. Many pulpits are filled with pastors and leaders who use people and destroy relationships because they are driven to fill emotional holes, prove themselves, mask the pain with success. The true need is for a father's affirmation—which is a hole too large for performance to fill.

The only way to break this orphan spirit is for people to be filled with a sense of the Father's love through Christ. That love, which is shed aboard in our hearts by the indwelling Holy Spirit (Rom. 5:5), enables us to become mature sons who serve God out of an overflow of love and vision rather than a need to earn respect or identity via performance.

The orphan spirit is the by-product of alienation from God

Sonship is not received by information, education, or even inspiration,
but by the revelation of the Holy Spirit

and thus the greatest curse on the earth today. A revelation of sonship that comes to the human spirit by the Holy Spirit is the only antidote to the orphan heart. Only when a person is healed of fatherlessness through the love of God is the orphan spirit displaced by the process of transforming sonship. Sonship is so important that all creation is presently crying out for the manifestation of the mature sons (*huios*) of God (Rom. 8:19).

Consider the kind of fruit that comes from orphan spirit and the spirit of sonship:

1. The orphan spirit promotes insecurity and jealousy. The spirit of sonship cultivates love and acceptance.

Without a deep revelation of sonship we are constantly battling jealousy and insecurity, since sonship is grounded in the identity of a father, a sense of home, and the security of an inheritance (Rom. 8:14-17). That security is to be transferred through loving parents who instill trust through love. The mistrust of an orphan heart produces such insecurity that hearing a biological or spiritual father praise one's siblings or co-laborer is difficult. But those with the spirit of sonship are so secure in the Father's love and favor that they're content to serve in any capacity needed, whether or not they are in charge or celebrated in the process.

2. The orphan spirit, driving a person to prove their worth and validate their identity, serves God in order to earn the Father's love. The mature son seeks to fulfill the Father's unfinished business in the atmosphere of divine acceptance and favor.

Those with an orphan spirit are constantly striving to earn the Father's love through accomplishment in ministry or career. Position, possessions, passions, and power seem to fill the emotional and spiritual holes, at least to medicate the pain. The orphan heart will substitute being in the presence of God for being in the presence of great men. Those with a spirit of sonship already know they are accepted in Christ and serve others out of the abundance of this acceptance (see John 13:1-5).

3. The orphan spirit is jealous of the success of his brothers. The mature son is committed to the success of his brothers and can serve freely since his own identity and worth is already secured.

Those with an orphan spirit are happy when their brother fails because it makes them feel better about themselves. The spirit of sonship, on the other hand, joyfully commits to serve, celebrate, and help their brothers succeed; since they have freely received they can freely give.

4. The orphan spirit tries to medicate the deep internal alienation through physical and emotional stimulation. The mature son walks in the joy and presence of the Lord for comfort.

Those with an orphan spirit are constantly trying to push down their sense of alienation, loneliness and lack of self-worth through work, temporary relationships, physical and emotional gratification and self-indulgence. However, the more one indulges the desires of the flesh, the more addicted the neurological pathways become. The Spirit of God works in the heart, mind and body of sons to restore integration and wholeness between spirit, soul, and body.

Sons get "re-wired" to the presence and love of God, which opens their spiritual ears to the Father's voice, and subsequently produces the antidote—the joy of the Lord—as their source of a son's strength.

5. The orphan spirit is driven by the need for success, affirmation, and the approval of men. In contrast, the Spirit leads the mature son into his calling and mission with humility.

Many attempt to accomplish great things to satisfy the deep yearning in their hearts for their father's approval (or to prove that father or authority figures were wrong about them). The most subtle of orphan lies is to use "biblical principles" as a way to achieve human success. This results in a drive to succeed as proof of God's blessing rather than being led by the Spirit. The results is confusing to the untrained eye. The outward appearance of growth and success often masks huge debt, unhealthy relationships, growing arrogance and self-centeredness. The idea that all material blessing is a sign of sonship is a snare for many young believers. The proof is seen in the many spiritual orphans in the world that don't know God and yet enjoy apparent wealth.

Sons, however, have discovered that "their life is hidden with Christ in God" (Col.3:3), the Father knows what they have need of without taking thought for it (Matt. 6:32-33), therefore they can focus on doing the Father's will, not their own. The motivation, the energizing power of sons, is doing the will of the Father. "My food (sustaining energy) is to do the will of him who sent me, and to finish His work" (John 4:34). Sons trust the Lord to direct them and bring opportunities to them without having to fabricate their own success.

6. The orphan spirit uses people as objects to achieve objectives. Mature sons serve people from a motivation of compassion because it's the Father's heart for His children.

Ray S. Anderson says, "We can either use the people to get the

Sonship is not received by information, education, or even inspiration, but by the revelation of the Holy Spirit

work done, or we can use the work to get the people done (matured and developed)." Those with an orphan spirit tend to use people as objects to accomplish their goals. They only have friends who serve a utilitarian purpose or make them feel better about themselves. Thus objectification and manipulation (threats and leverages) are used to control.

Sons are always about the Father's business, which is to redeem, restore, and affirm others so they can rise to the Father's purpose for their life. Sons can "wash other's feet" in true service because they know where they came from and where they are going, and thus have nothing to prove and nothing to lose (John 13:1-5). Sons don't use people; they serve and release people to fulfill their destiny in Christ.

7. The orphan spirit is often revealed in fits of anger and rage. The spirit of sonship rests in the Father's ability to "make what was meant for evil to turn to our good.

The orphan spirit produces uncontrollable anger, fits of rage and even violence because its best efforts are rooted in a cause-and-effect world of controlling God, others, and circumstances. To the orphan heart, religion (spiritual protocols of right vs wrong behavior) is a way to force God's hand to get what one wants. If I do the right things, God must compensate. These emotional outbursts of frustration only reveal

a lack the trust in the Father's incomparable love—His tenacious desire to give His children the kingdom, not on the basis of merit but mercy.

Those walking in sonship learn a way of rest (Matt. 11:28) and have ceased from their own works so the Father can have His way in their lives. This is not to be confused with a qué será será, "whatever will be will be", but with an awareness of the greatness and unfathomable wisdom of God to know what is best for His child because He is committed to nothing less than the best for His sons and daughters.

8. The orphan spirit breeds competition with others. Sonship blesses others.

The orphan spirit, due to insecurity, lives in a world of comparisons. It places a high value on "being the best"—whether in business, the church, family, or even recreation. This is easily camouflaged in terminology of the American dream or "whatever one can conceive one can achieve" (i.e. humanism). Christ is an unrealistic measure or model to the orphan, so comparison to others is the holy grail.

Those who walk in sonship are constantly seeing how they can bless others since they already have the affirmation of God in their souls. The competition of sons is "the competition of generosity"— seeing who can bless the other the most (also the best recipe for a

Sonship is not received by information, education, or even inspiration, but by the revelation of the Holy Spirit

healthy marriage). Sons know they will never lack anything they need since, in the giving of the Father's only Son, He has freely given everything (Rom. 8:32; 1 Cor. 3:21-22). Sons discover that the more they are filled with the Spirit, the more they want to freely share with others.

9. The orphan spirit is driven by impulsiveness. The spirit of sonship walks in the eternal sense of timelessness and peace.

In the need to prove it's worth, the orphan heart is susceptible to bargaining and time pressure. Impulsive decisions and "get rich quick schemes" are the common landmines of the orphan soul. "If I don't act now, I will miss out on the deal of a lifetime." "I know we can't afford it right now, but we can get a loan and God will help us …." "I just feel better about myself when I buy new stuff …." "I deserve it as much as anyone else …." The orphan heart finds its identity in external symbols of success and struggles to patiently wait on God.

Those walking in sonship are filled with a sense of divine love, acceptance, and provision. They learn that they can be content in whatever circumstance they may be in, whether having little or much (Phil. 4:11-12), because their life does not consist of the abundance of things one possesses (Luke 12:15). This sense of supernatural care frees sons from the pressure to prove worth by outward possessions and symbols of success. Sons are led by an internal sense of "peace which surpasses all understanding" (Phil. 4:7). Orphans are driven with impulsiveness, sons are led with peace "beside still waters."

10. The orphan spirit perceives God as far away and difficult to access. The spirit of sonship is grounded in a daily intimate relationship with the indwelling Holy Spirit who never leaves us and is always speaking.

The orphan heart cannot grasp the unconditional love of the Father, nor that a perfect Father would want to be with man, even in his imperfections. The orphan heart will either use religion to build a ladder upon which self-effort climbs to God (do the right things), or it will accuse God of His seeming absence. The orphan lie is that "God was not there when bad things happened," or "If He is good, why did He let this happen?" The compliant orphan will work dutifully within the religious box; the defiant orphan with live life on his own terms, shaking a fist at God. But he cannot believe that God is always near.

The revelation of sonship includes, among other things, the revelation that "I will never leave you nor forsake you." That is, "I am with you and I am forever for you." Sons understand that the Holy Spirit lives inside, is forming "the *Abba* cry" within them to convince

*Sonship is not received by information, education, or even inspiration,
but by the revelation of the Holy Spirit*

their orphan heart and mind of the Father's constant presence. The orphan heart sings "prove to me that You are near." The son sings, "I will never be alone again."

In conclusion, the greatest gift known to humankind is to accept, receive and walk in the love of the Father, who so loved the world that He gave His only Son so that we may not perish or waste our lives away but experience the abundant life that only our divine Father can give.

This article is adapted and significantly edited by Dr. Kerry Wood from the original by Joseph Mattera, presiding bishop of Christ Covenant Coalition and the overseeing Bishop of Resurrection Church in New York. He is the author of four theological books on the kingdom of God, entitled Ruling in the Gates (2003), Kingdom Revolution (2009), Kingdom Awakening (2010) and Walk in Generational Blessings (2012).

• •

Personal Reflection

What is the Lord saying to you?

Sonship is not received by information, education, or even inspiration, but by the revelation of the Holy Spirit

Week 6

The Progression to an Orphan Spirit (cont'd)

Meditation Verse

> **Now may the God of peace Himself sanctify you completely; and may your whole spirit, soul, and body be preserved blameless at the coming of our Lord Jesus Christ. (1 Thess. 5:23)**

The verse in context:

> *Throw out anything tainted with evil. May God himself, the God who makes everything holy and whole, make you holy and whole, put you together—spirit, soul, and body—and keep you fit for the coming of our Master, Jesus Christ. The One who called you is completely dependable. If he said it, he'll do it!*
> 1 Thessalonians 5:22-24, The Message

Assigned Reading: *The Abba Factor*, Chapter 6

Chapter Summary

Ultimately, because we are made in the image and likeness of a relational three-and-one God (Trinity), everything about us is designed for relational wholeness. The enemy's desire is to fracture us, first within ourselves, so that our spirit and mind are at war with the other. Then our internal (inner personal) dis-integration becomes interpersonal disintegration. We are willing to settle for superficial relationships because we've believed a lie that no one would love us if they really knew us. Either "I am not lovable, or they are not lovable"—and both are a lie.

That lie gets reinforced by self-fulfilling rejection of others which produces a stronghold that says, "I'm on my own"—self-reliance (or the other extreme is victimization). We soothe the pain of our loneliness with counterfeit affections.

In the end, those lies come with re-defined terms so that right seems wrong and wrong seems right.

Sonship is not received by information, education, or even inspiration, but by the revelation of the Holy Spirit

Questions:

1) What does James 1:14-15 tell us about how strongholds get established in our lives?

2) What are some of the reasons why we are willing to settle for superficial relationships when we are designed to experience real intimacy?

3) How have you seen the stronghold thought that says, "I'm on my own," play out in different situations? In what way have you felt that yourself?

4) Name some ways we see the "terms" being redefined in our culture to make the strongholds of either self-reliance or victimization acceptable.

5) Look back through Chapters 5 and 6: recount the progressive nature of a person's alienation from self, others and God by listing numbers 1 through 12 of the Orphan Progression. Which of these spoke most clearly to you?

• •

Supplemental Article

Identity Crisis Can Have Life or Death Consequences

The following is a Reuters news article by Cheryl Platzman Weinstock (March 15, 2018) writing for Reuters. It reveals that upcoming generations are struggling more and more with an identity crisis that leaves them with little hope and a susceptibility to suicide. The orphan spirit seeks to steal, kill, and destroy with an ultimate aim to forever separate us from the Father's love. "Sexual orientation" is the glamour term for identity confusion, which is the result of a fatherless generation. Is this not the most critical time in history for orphans to be reconciled to the Father by a message of sonship?

Sexual Orientation Top Risk for Suicidal Thoughts in College Freshmen

A study done by the University of Belgium in 2015 found that nearly one third of first-year college students have thought about suicide, according to a study across eight countries, and non-heterosexual identity or feelings were the biggest risks for this kind of thinking or behavior.

Having a religion other than Christianity, being female, having unmarried parents or at least one deceased parent and being age 20 or older were also important risk factors, though being a sexual minority also carried the highest risk of transitioning from suicidal thoughts to plans to attempts, the researchers found.

"It is important to realize … that the relative increase in risk is still modest," said lead author Philippe Mortier, a neuroscience researcher at Leuven University in Belgium. "Especially when we consider suicide attempts (with a lifetime prevalence of 4.3 percent), it is important to keep in mind that most students who struggle with sexual orientation issues will not develop serious suicidality," he said by email.

"It is therefore important that future studies take into account

Sonship is not received by information, education, or even inspiration, but by the revelation of the Holy Spirit

a higher number of additional risk and protective factors to better differentiate which particular students in high-risk groups will go on and commit attempts and eventually suicide," Mortier added.

Globally, suicide was the second leading cause of death among 15- to 29-year-olds in 2015, according to the World Health Organization (WHO). The study team analyzed data from the WHO World Mental Health Surveys International College Student Project, including responses from a total of 13,984 first-year college students at seven private and 12 public institutions in Australia, Belgium, Germany, Mexico, Northern Ireland, South Africa, Spain and the U.S.

Although the lifetime prevalence of suicidal thinking or behaviors varied by country, ranging from 15 percent to almost 45 percent, the age of onset and persistence of suicidality as well as the risk factors were very similar among all late adolescents, the authors note.

Overall, half of the participants were 19 years old or younger, and 32.7 percent reported ever having thought about taking their own lives. A subset of 17.5 percent had made plans for how they would commit suicide and 4.3 percent had made an actual attempt. Three quarters of these students reported having first had suicidal thoughts by the time they were 16 years old.

More than half (53 percent) of those who had thought about it made the transition to a suicide plan. Approximately 22 percent of those who had made a plan transitioned to making a suicide attempt.

The study team found that sexual minorities, such as lesbian, gay, bisexual and transgender (LGBT) students were at four-to-eight-fold higher risk than others for suicidal thoughts and behaviors. Heterosexual students with experience of same-sex intercourse were at about three-to-four-fold higher risk, while heterosexual students with same-sex attraction had about double the risk.

Other factors like non-Christian religion, age and parental characteristics raised risk by about two-fold or less. Sexual orientation also raised the likelihood of transitioning from suicidal thinking to plans or attempts by up to three-fold.

"Some people worry that this data may stigmatize sexual minorities," said Jacqueline Pistorello, a clinical psychologist and researcher at the University of Nevada, Reno's counseling services, who wasn't involved in the study. "Suicidality has multiple pathways. We need to focus on what are the skills we need to give these kids to keep them alive," she said in a telephone interview.

Among the study's limitations are low response rates in some countries, and the fact that participants might not be as forthcoming about suicidal thinking in an online survey as in an interview with another person, the authors note. In addition, the study highlights associations but cannot prove that certain risk factors directly cause suicidal thoughts or tendencies.

The study team writes in the Journal of the American Academy of Child and Adolescent Psychiatry, "Maybe this study will get the attention of a university administrator who will see the suicide problem as not just at their school, but widespread and it may elevate their level of awareness," said Victor Schwartz, chief medical officer at the JED Foundation in New York, which targets the mental health of young adults, who wasn't involved in the current research.

This is not an endorsement of the conclusions or implications of either the author of the article or the researcher team. This information reveals the deep issues that stem from a lack of identity, and especially the impacts of father wounds (see *The Abba Factor*, p 30-31, Lee Strobel's story).

www.reuters.com/article/us-health-college-suicide/sexual-orientation-top-risk-for-suicidal-thoughts-in-college-freshmen-idUSKCN1GR34X

• •

Personal Reflection

What is the Lord saying to you?

Sonship is not received by information, education, or even inspiration,
but by the revelation of the Holy Spirit

Week 7
Fake Fullness:
Accepting Counterfeits as Real

Meditation Verse

> *For in Christ all the fullness of the Deity lives in bodily form, and in Christ you have been brought to fullness.*
> *(Col 2:9-10)*

The verse in context:

> *See to it that no one takes you captive through hollow and deceptive philosophy, which depends on human tradition and the elemental spiritual forces of this world rather than on Christ.*
> *For in Christ all the fullness of the Deity lives in bodily form, and in Christ you have been brought to fullness. He is the head over every power and authority. In him you were also circumcised with a circumcision not performed by human hands. Your whole self ruled by the flesh was put off when you were circumcised by Christ.*
> Colossians 2:8-11, NIV

Assigned Reading: *The Abba Factor*, Chapter 7

Chapter Summary

We are made in God's image as relational beings designed to live in overflowing fullness. Man was designed to be filled and stay filled in the relational connection of worship—not because God needs our worship, but because He designed us in His image, to thrive in relationship and to receive of His perpetual overflowing fullness. Jesus' own ministry demonstrated the Father's desire for our fullness (pp. 87-88).

Satan's end-game is to offer various versions of fullness—"fake fullness"—in an effort to ultimately separate us from the Father's love (and thwart the Father's loving purpose). We are certain of two realities about Satan's tactics: first, Satan uses (and plays upon) our God-given drives to bring confusion between The Source and resources. Secondly, every temptation we will ever face is designed to challenge our identity—to get us to doubt our sonship.

Orphans will settle for fullness-substitutes of passions, possessions, position and power—each of these intoxicate like a drug.

Sonship is not received by information, education, or even inspiration,
but by the revelation of the Holy Spirit

Sons live in the fullness of the Father's love and know that the power of Christ rests upon us when we are neither moved by weakness or strength, but by immediate obedience to the Father. God is the only Source, everything else is resource. Sons carry an awareness of an eternal future, which protects them from the impulsiveness of the now.

Questions:

1) What are some verses of Scripture that reveal that we were made for fullness?

2) What is Satan's primary target in his business of temptation? Is it more than sinning?

3) What example can you think of in your own life where passions, possessions, position, or power have been a substitute for real fullness in God?

4) Think about the four types of Fake-fullness: passion of the flesh, possessions, position, and power. In what ways do these make us "feel" good about ourselves and serve as substitutes for our true identity?

Sonship is not received by information, education, or even inspiration,
but by the revelation of the Holy Spirit

5) Which of these four types of "Fake-fullness" identify your primary battle ground—where the enemy tempts you to perform for proof that you are valuable?

6) . How would your life be different if you were totally unafraid of what others thought about you, or you had nothing to prove to anyone?

• •

Supplemental Article

Approval Addiction and Identity
by Matt Russell

After I experienced some sobriety from my primary addiction it became clear that there were a lot of other processes that I was addicted to—ways of thinking and acting that fed my main addiction. One of those sub-addictions ran deep underneath the radar of my life. It has nothing to do with chemical dependency or substance abuse. There are no twelve-step groups to help people fight it. There are no treatment centers to help us escape it. But for a lot of us it creates relational, spiritual and social havoc in our lives.

This particular addiction is what might be called approval addiction. It involves people living in bondage to what other people think about us. When you become an addict to approval, no matter how much of

this drug of choice you get, you can never have enough. You've got to have more and more and more fixes and, like other junkies, you can go crazy when your drug of choice is withheld.

My personal experience with approval addiction began early. When I was in elementary school I used to talk a lot (for folks that know me that will be a real shocker!). There were all these rules about being quiet, studying, and listening that I had a difficult time with. I found the little folks around me fascinating and so I would talk to them all the time. My second-grade teacher was not impressed by my social skills. Over time it became obvious that she had her favorites and I wasn't one of them. I tried to make her like me but it was useless.

Sonship is not received by information, education, or even inspiration,
but by the revelation of the Holy Spirit

One day I was particularly fascinated by the folks around me—and so she pulled me out of class and spanked me. The next day I was determined to do better. By the end of the day she asked me to come forward and she pinned a note on my shirt and told me to make sure it got to my mother. I just knew that it was going to be a glowing report of how much progress I had made in that eight-hour period. I was sure that the note was going to enumerate how in all the years of teaching she had never seen a turn around so inspirational or dramatic. That is not what happened. When I got home I stuck my chest out and told my mom that I got a note from my teacher—I was confident, I was proud, I knew I was loved.

As my mom read the note and as her continence fell, so did mine. The note said that I was a very bad boy and it went on to inventory all my seven year old character defects. Which, from the length of time it took my mom to read the note, was pretty long.

That is the first time I remember feeling significantly criticized and it crushed me. It took the air out of my sails. This sense of shame bubbled up from the bottom and it made me feel small and insignificant. Criticism still does that to me. I think that there was a part of me that day that determined never to feel that way again—to distance myself, to people please, to manipulate and lie—but to never feel that

way again. In a lot of ways the structure and life of my addiction served to numb me from the shame of letting people down. Today I can see the insanity of this logic (doing shameful things to numb my shame)—but it made all the sense in the world to me at the time.

Those of us who struggle with this often have no capacity to hear criticism. We hide from it, balk at it, internalize it, and strike back at the originators of it. When other people's opinion of me becomes the organizing principle of my life my entire identity is on the line. What happens is that I end up giving people access to my identity that should not have that access. I become what other people think of me. Whether I am a student, a businessman, a stay at home mom, a professional, or unemployed, whether I'm a recovering addict, a Christian, a Democrat or Republican, successful—it doesn't matter. The only thing that matters is how I am perceived by my world. If being busy is important, then I must be busy. If having money is a sign of real freedom, then I must claim my money. If knowing people proves my importance, I will have to work my contacts and climb the ladders. What matters is how I am perceived by my world.

I have seen a spiritual principle at work in my sobriety in relationship to this: Living in the gracious acceptance and approval of God will liberate me from the

Sonship is not received by information, education, or even inspiration, but by the revelation of the Holy Spirit

approval addiction. The converse is true too. Living as an approval addict will keep me from living in the love of God. May you live in the overwhelming, saturating love and acceptance of God.

(with permission) Matt Russell writes for The National Association for Christian Recovery. NACR, 563 Southlake Blvd., Richmond, VA 23236 http://www.nacr. org/families/resources-for-codependents/ approval-addiction-and-identity

• •

Personal Reflection

What is the Lord saying to you?

Week 8

Transformation: Turned into Another Man

Meditation Verse

> ***May you be filled though all your being with God himself!***
> ***(Eph. 3:19, J.B. Philips)***

The verse in context:

> *I pray that out of the glorious richness of his resources he will enable you to know*
> *the strength of the spirit's inner re-enforcement—that Christ may actually live*
> *in your hearts by your faith. And I pray that you, firmly fixed in love yourselves,*
> *may be able to grasp (with all Christians) how wide and deep and long and*
> *high is the love of Christ—and to know for yourselves that love so far beyond our*
> *comprehension. May you be filled through all your being with God himself!*
>
> Ephesians 3:16-19, J.B. Philips

Assigned Reading: *The Abba Factor*, Chapter 8

Chapter Summary

Saul, as the first King of Israel, becomes a type—revealing that anointing alone is not enough to rule. There is a necessary process of transformation which prepares us to walk in the Spirit-partnered rulership afforded Sons. Saul, fairly clueless to God's greater purposes for his life, submits to a divine encounter with the prophet, which leads to a series of divinely appointed experiences designed to prepare him for this high calling. The anointing oil immediately points to the role/work of the Holy Spirit in the transformation process. It's the Holy Spirit who transforms us into the Lord's purposes for us.

The Lord's purpose is to restore us to our place of sonship—as "captains over the Lord's inheritance"— that inheritance is first and foremost the people of God themselves. God has chosen us, His people, as His inheritance.

The anointing is followed by a series of transformational encounters prescribed to reset our compass, calibrate our consciousness, to a life and destiny of reining as kings. We see through Saul's encounters that each of us would have similar "gaps" in understanding who we really are and why God would use us. *The Abba Factor* is seen here as the Holy Spirit's releasing you from the tyranny of sadness, self-importance, and self-accusation that will keep you from fulfilling the Father's call to rule in the Son.

Sonship is not received by information, education, or even inspiration,
but by the revelation of the Holy Spirit

Questions:

1) What does Saul's anointing and journey to coronation tell you about the process of transformation to sonship (1 Samuel 10 and 11)?

2) What are the points of personal encounter Saul had to experience before he could rule as a king?

3) Which of these—the tyranny of sadness, self-importance, or self-accusation—are most like your own journey?

4) Who can you talk to (the God-ordained relationships in your life) about these areas of accountability (disappointment, sadness, pride, shame) and "heart checks" for "the cutting away of the flesh" (sanctification)?

5) Reflect on any divinely appointed experiences you have had that were transformational moments for you? Name something God did in you to set you free from an area of personal bondage or a lie you believed about yourself (also use "reflection page" after the article)

Sonship is not received by information, education, or even inspiration, but by the revelation of the Holy Spirit

Supplemental Article

The Truth About Transformation

Transformation that begins at the cognitive thinking level is a myth at worst, short-lived at best. All the bravado talk of "change your thinking and you change your life" ultimately falls short because it fails to acknowledge that the deepest part of man is not the mind, but the spirit. Human beings are fundamentally eternal, spirit-beings. If it is true that "out of the heart flows the forces of life" (Pr. 4:23), and "out of the abundance of the heart (not the mind) the mouth speaks" (Matt. 12:34), then the starting point for transformation is not at the cognitive level, not even at the subconscious level (in the psychological sense), but at the spirit level. The spirit of man is that part of man that connects and communicates with the Spirit of God and the spiritual world.

If this sounds far-fetched and out of reach, one must only consider Jesus' words that He would send the Holy Spirit to those who believe in Him, and the Spirit would bear witness in our hearts (spirit) to a new reality, and would connect us to the heart, mind and will of God (see John 14 and 16). Thus, real transformation begins with a new heart (Ezek. 36 and John 3). But that is only the first step of an ongoing process.

Transformation is an integrated process that includes and combines 1.) the supernatural energizing power of the Holy Spirit (in a person's spirit), 2.) the harnessing of Spirit-energized experiences to replace traumatic experiences (emotions and memory), and 3.) the reinforcing of the new being and knowing into repetitive habits of victory (behavior). Ultimately, at its most basic components, transformation involves being, believing, and behaving. True transformation isn't realized until all three parts of a person are re-aligned into an integrated wholeness or unity—so that what I believe is aligned to who I really am (being), and what I do (behavior) is aligned to what I really believe. To say it another way, I am whole when my behavior flows out of my believing, and what I believe flows out of who I "be". A transformed person is whole spirit, mind and body; their being, believing and behaving all flow from the same place.

Does this raise the question in your mind, "How can I believe something that is different from who I really am?" Of course, this is how the lies of the enemy work. For example, Jesus' wilderness temptations by Satan were all to one end—to get the Son of God to doubt that He was the Son. "If you be the son of God ... then prove it ..." (my paraphrase). The reason Jesus sent the Holy Spirit into our hearts was to convince us (our minds/our believing) of who we really are as new creations in Christ.

---

*Sonship is not received by information, education, or even inspiration,
but by the revelation of the Holy Spirit*

Why doesn't positive mental attitude work? Humanism attempts to control thoughts, behavior and circumstances by programming positive thoughts at the cognitive level. The power of positive thinking is only powerful until crisis (extreme pressures) shines a light of the difference between who we really are and what we believe about our true self. So we attempt to muster identity by building a paper tower of thoughts, "I am the captain of my own fate." "I can do anything. "Whatever I can conceive, I can achieve. "Nothing can stop me. Nothing can hold me back. My own will is always within my control." "Man becomes what he believes himself to be."

These all sound good, and even contain kernels of truth. The problem is, the heart is deceitful and inherently wicked until it is made new in Jesus Christ. I can flood my mind with positive thoughts, but if the sub-structure, the spirit, is wicked or broken, it will continue to want/desire things that bring self-destruction. There is a way that seems right, but leads to death. The destructive disconnect between our spirit and mind is discovered in the lies that we have believed about ourselves. And rehearsing a mantra of positive thoughts at the cognitive level won't displace what we believe at the deeper, spiritual level. It is only a band aid, a thin veneer that masks the lie until pressure comes, and like a slow volcanic eruption, the hot lava begins breaking through the fractures and fissures of the surface. What is the answer?

First, we must be made new at the deepest place, what the Apostle Peter calls "the hidden man of the heart" (1 Pet. 3:4) and the Apostle Paul calls "the inner man" (Eph. 3:16). A leopard can't change his own spots and man cannot change his own spirit. Only God, by His Spirit, can come in and transform a man from the inside out, so that old things are passed away, and all things become new (2 Cor. 5:17). This is the first step that opens the door for a person to enter into a new world of spiritual life, where spiritual death is displaced with life in the deepest part of one's being.

In short, it is by the Father's voice in our spirits (an ongoing daily conversation of intimacy and empowering) that we receive the power in **our inner man**, which creates and energizes our **will** (by the Spirit in our spirit), to establish **new habits** and re-wire the circuitry of the brain to live consistently victorious and overflowing lives. Jesus called this "abiding". Any "formula" for personal transformation that is not rooted in the daily renewal of our inward man (spirit) by abiding in the Voice and Presence of God, will eventually be reduced to best efforts of will power.

*See **The Abba Formation** by Kerry Wood for in-depth treatment of the process of transformation.*

Sonship is not received by information, education, or even inspiration, but by the revelation of the Holy Spirit

Personal Reflection

What is the Lord saying to you?

Week 9

The Progression of the Spirit of Sonship

Meditation Verse

Now may the God of peace ... make you complete in every good work to do His will, working in you what is well pleasing in His sight, through Jesus Christ, to whom be glory forever and ever. Amen. (Hebrews 13:20-21)

The verse in context:

May God, who puts all things together, makes all things whole, Who made a lasting mark through the sacrifice of Jesus, the sacrifice of blood that sealed the eternal covenant, Who led Jesus, our Great Shepherd, up and alive from the dead, Now put you together, provide you with everything you need to please him, Make us into what gives him most pleasure, by means of the sacrifice of Jesus, the Messiah. All glory to Jesus forever and always! Oh, yes, yes, yes.

Hebrews 13:19-21, The Message

Assigned Reading: *The Abba Factor*, Chapter 9

Chapter Summary

If there is a progression into the orphan spirit, it stands to reason that there is also a progression into a full awareness and lifestyle of sonship. Paul admonishes the Romans (and us) to be transformed (metamorphosed) by the renewing of our mind (Rom. 12:2). In other words, a radical change came to our spirits by the new birth, and now there is a process involved in getting our thinking aligned to our new identity as sons. The Apostle John says, "Now are we sons of God, though it doesn't totally look like it yet" (1 John 3:3 *my paraphrase*) or, as The Message says, "... *and that's only the beginning!*"

The first part of the progression from orphan to son looks something like this:

If Satan begins the orphan attack by disappointed expectations from those in authority (e.g. fathers and mothers), then the Divine reversal would involve God fulfilling expectations; better yet, refocusing our expectations in God. Getting our eyes back on the Good Father means the Holy Spirit begins to show us that we are totally accepted by this God of Love who is willing to come be with us in the middle of our mess. This revelation of love leads to a restoration of trust, which empowers me to forgive. This forgiveness is

Sonship is not received by information, education, or even inspiration, but by the revelation of the Holy Spirit

not in-word-only, but includes "a double-barrel" work of choosing to forgive and learning to pro-actively pray and bless those we are forgiving (see the Supplemental Reading).

As we are discipled more and more to the Father's voice we begin to experience a faith that comes by hearing the (*rhema*) Word in our spirit (Rom. 10:17). This faith enables us to walk into a restoration of vulnerability in trust and security. In the awareness of sonship—having nothing to hide, prove, fear or lose—we move from an independent, self-reliant mindset to one who is giving and receiving in community. Note how wholeness begins to reintegrate us spirit, soul, and body. This isn't a compartmentalized religion, but a new man shining through.

Questions:

1) Have you had the idea that you could be right with God and yet ignore broken relationships or personal stuff we lock away in a closet of our shameful memories? Reflect on any broken or hidden thing that the Holy Spirit might bring to your mind (and write them down).

2) What are some of the ways we see ourselves or others still trying to measure up, perform, or hide?

3) Turn to Hebrews 13:5-6. What can you glean from this passage that helps us understand something of our role in this transformation?

4) Talk about the two facets of "the double barrel" of forgiveness—both choosing to forgive/release and proactively and intentionally blessing the person that offended us?

5) Look at the first "Six Steps" of the sonship progression. Which one(s) still seems difficult for you?

• •

Supplemental Article

Avoiding Transformation
Short-circuiting the Process

Real transformation is a multi-layered process that is interacting at a spirit (*pneuma*), soul (*psuche*), and physical (soma) level. We were designed as a wholeness—a oneness—but the separation of sin caused a fragmentation within that the Father is out to restore. We could say we be (in spirit), we believe (in soul), and we behave (in body). But with all God has offered, we find ways to avoid the transformation of our pain. Consider:

The Fighter—Fighters are looking for the evildoer, the sinner, the unjust one, the oppressor, the bad person "over there." He or she "righteously" attacks, hates, or even kills the wrong-doer, while feeling heroic for doing so (see John 16:2). We are all tempted to project our problem on someone or something else rather than dealing with it in ourselves.

The Zealot—and we've all been one at different times—is actually relieved by having someone to hate, because it takes away our inner shame and anxiety and provides a false sense of innocence. As long as the evil is "over there" and we can keep our focus on changing or expelling someone else (as the contaminating element), then we feel at peace. But this is not the peace of Christ, which "the world cannot give" (see John 14:27).

*Sonship is not received by information, education, or even inspiration,
but by the revelation of the Holy Spirit*

The Victim—playing the victim is another way to deal with pain indirectly. You blame someone else, and your pain becomes your personal ticket to power because it gives you a false sense of moral superiority and outrage. You don't have to grow up, let go, forgive, or surrender—you just have to accuse someone else of being worse than you are. And sadly, that becomes your very fragile identity, which always needs more reinforcement.

Flight and Denial—The other common way to avoid the path of transformation is the way of flight or denial.. Those with the instinct to flee will often deny or ignore pain by naively dividing the world into purity codes and worthiness systems. They keep the problem on the level of words, ideas, and absolute laws separating good and evil. They refuse to live in the real world of complexity. They divide the world into good guys and bad guys, a comfortable but false world of black and white. It is always others who must be excluded so I can be pure and holy. Denial is an understandable—but false—way of coping. Yet it is often the only way that many people can deal with the complexity of their human situation.

All of these patterns perpetuate pain and violence rather than bringing true healing. Jesus took the more difficult path: to know the depths of suffering and sin and yet to forgive reality for being what it is. It is equally hard to trust both sides—the dying itself and the promised new creation. It is only possible by the Person from Heaven who lives in you—the Holy Spirit. He knows you better than you know yourself, and He can get you aligned—being, believing, and behaving as the son/daughter of the Father that you are. You do realize that a Person from Heaven lives in you, don't you?

Personal Reflection

What is the Lord saying to you?

Sonship is not received by information, education, or even inspiration, but by the revelation of the Holy Spirit

Week 10

The Progression of the Spirit of Sonship (cont'd)

Meditation Verse

> *For it is [not your strength, but it is] God who is effectively at work in you, both to will and to work [that is, strengthening, energizing, and creating in you the longing and the ability to fulfill your purpose] for His good pleasure. (Phil 2:13, AMP)*

The verse in context:

> *So then, my dear ones, just as you have always obeyed [my instructions with enthusiasm], not only in my presence, but now much more in my absence, continue to work out your salvation [that is, cultivate it, bring it to full effect, actively pursue spiritual maturity] with awe-inspired fear and trembling [using serious caution and critical self-evaluation to avoid anything that might offend God or discredit the name of Christ]. For it is not your strength, but it is God who is effectively at work in you, both to will and to work [that is, strengthening, energizing, and creating in you the longing and the ability to fulfill your purpose] for His good pleasure.*
>
> Philippians 2:12-13, AMP

Assigned Reading: *The Abba Factor*, Chapter 10

Chapter Summary

The progressive work of the Spirit starts with resetting expectations and broken trust and ends with a fullness that propels sons and daughters to live in full freedom of the Father's blessing. What Satan has broken and distorted in us by the orphan progression, the Holy Spirit restores through the *Abba* Cry. It looks like this:

- Divinely fulfilled expectations: where our expectations are only in God, to
- A revelation that we are accepted in the beloved, to
- Restored trust experienced in the power to forgive and bless those that wound us, to
- A spirit of faith that comes through the spoken, experiential hearing of the Word of God, to

Sonship is not received by information, education, or even inspiration, but by the revelation of the Holy Spirit

125

- The vulnerability of a totally trusting, secure son, to
- Move from an independent spirit to an inter-dependent spirit, to
- Honoring others in their gifts, callings and differences, to
- Relational intimacy experienced in fellowship (Koinonia), to
- Receiving our thoughts and appetites from the Spirit, to
- Learning to live in the overflow of Spirit Fullness, to
- Speaking the Truth in love and worship in Spirit and Truth, to
- Living by the power of the Spirit—the Triune Life of God.

Jesus came as a Son to show us how we could live, here and now, by the same indwelling Holy Spirit—and He lived this way among us. If it seems impossible to our mind, yes, it is impossible for us, but not God. This is what the Holy Spirit is actively doing in those who will make space for Him to speak and work daily.

Questions:

1) Which of these feel way out of reach to you at this point?

2) Can you allow others to be at a different place in God than you?

3) Do you feel you are still trying to become something else, or do you sense God is showing you who you already are in Him?

4) To what degree do you feel you must defend God—fight for the "right?"

5) If you have read the "supplemental article" **Process of Transformation**, what's the ultimate purpose of our transformation?

• •

Supplemental Article

The Process of Transformation

Rest—> Reflection—>Revelation—>Renovation

Every breakthrough (**renovation**) has been preceded by a **revelation** from God, which was prefaced by deep **reflection**, which came from **rest**. Jesus' own life is demonstration of the transformation process on numerous levels. Whether Moses, John the Baptist, Jesus, or the Apostle John on the isle of Patmos, the process is essentially the same.

> *Jesus said to them, Except a kernel of wheat fall into the ground and die, it abides alone: but if it die, it brings forth much fruit. He that loves his life shall lose it; and he that hates his life in this world shall keep it unto life eternal.*
>
> John 12:23

Jesus says this immediately after coming from Mary's house where they were celebrating Lazarus' being raised from the dead (John 12:1-2). But what is on His mind is his entrance into Jerusalem to lay His life down. He is personally in a circumstantial vortex of death and resurrection; Lazarus' death and resurrection, and now His own. This raising of Lazarus is one of many illustrations in Scripture of transformation as *rest—reflection—revelation—renovation*.

Rest: When Lazarus was sick Mary and Martha sent word to Jesus so that He would come heal their brother—but strangely, Jesus delays His coming. Jesus tells his disciples that Lazarus "sleeps" (*rests*), but finally tells them plainly "He is dead" (John 11:4, 5; 11-14). Jesus then says what sounds possibly uncaring to us, "Lazarus is dead, and for your sake I am glad I was not there, so that you may believe " Jesus seems to be resting, not hurried. He is bringing His disciples to transformation through God-encounters that transform their thinking, first at the believing level.

Reflection: These four days that Lazarus is in the tomb represents rest that leads to *reflection*. Reflection opens a window to see that we need an encounter with God. Mary and Martha had been reflecting in mourning the loss of Lazarus, and it is easy to see the impact of their reflection: "Jesus, if you had been here your friend would not have died. We don't know what else to do."

Reflection uncovers all our lies, assumptions, misconceptions about ourselves and God. Reflection brings us face to face with our inability to produce in and of ourselves. Without reflection we will go on believing we can get by on our own—that everything we possess came from our own hands. Sabbath is the gift of resting for the purpose of reflection. Even God rested on the seventh day and reflecting on his work—that it was good.

Reflection has produced an urgency in Martha and Mary. They are using every emotional string they know to pull to get Jesus to move on their time table. They are

sure they know how God needs to work this out. "Lord, if you would have been here, my brother would not have died," (John 11:21). But the guilt trip is not enough. Within Martha is a desire to control God, to push God's levers to have her way, "But even now I know that God will give you whatever you ask," (11:22). We will make deals with God in the times between rest and revelation, because we are not in revelation yet; we do not yet see what God is trying to do.

Revelation. After Martha's somewhat ungrateful greeting Jesus says, "Your brother will rise again." Notice that reflection time is over, the revelation season is beginning. She counters, "Oh, I know he will rise in the resurrection." And Jesus drops a revelation bombshell, "I am the resurrection and the life. The one who believes in Me will live even though he die. Do you believe this?" And Jesus wept.

Do you see what Jesus is really after? Lazarus' death (loss, sorrow, denial) is on their minds. Now possible resurrection is on Martha's mind, but Jesus is after something greater. He wants to bring his disciples (certainly this includes Martha and Mary) to a revelation of who He is. "I am the resurrection and the life ... do you believe this?"

He is not asking if she can grasp this mentally. He is not saying, "Do you have theological space for this in your mental

Sonship is not received by information, education, or even inspiration, but by the revelation of the Holy Spirit

understanding of God?" Jesus is saying, "Resurrection (or healing, or answered prayer, etc.) is not just an event that helps you escape your temporary pain. **Resurrection is a Person**. I am that person, and having a person is better than having a great memory (the event)." Jesus is bringing Martha (and the rest of the disciples that experience the glory of God in the raising of Lazarus) to a place of knowing who God is, knowing His nature of loving redemption, knowing God as victor over death. Jesus is revealing to His disciples that His Father is not the death-dealing, judgmental, rule-keeping God they thought they knew from the Law and Prophets. It's a new day of revelation.

Renovation. We could use the word *repentance* (to think differently, to go a different way) except that it carries too much baggage in our minds. Jesus prays out loud in front of Lazarus' tomb, but not because he needs to pray, but so they will believe. Then he cries out, "Lazarus, come out of there!" He's still bound head to toe in grave clothes, so he doesn't walk out—he just comes out. This is a renovation on many levels. Lazarus was certainly renovated! But there was a renovation of minds, hearts, physical limitation, gravity … and what was the goal?

Every transformation is initially for the sake of the transformed. Lazarus is alive! Celebration for us! But that was temporary—Lazarus would die again one day. But the people saw God for who He really is! God is alive! Celebrate God! A loving *Abba* who comes running to His sons and daughters, without judgment, without a stone in His hand. They saw God weep at the tomb of a man that day.

● ●

Personal Reflection

What is the Lord saying to you?

Week 11
From Orphans to Heirs

Meditation Verse

> *Every good gift and every perfect gift is from above,*
> *and comes down from the Father of lights, with whom*
> *there is no variation or shadow of turning.(James 1:17)*

The verse in context:

> *So, my very dear friends, don't get thrown off course. Every desirable*
> *and beneficial gift comes out of heaven. The gifts are rivers of light*
> *cascading down from the Father of Light. There is nothing deceitful in*
> *God, nothing two-faced, nothing fickle. He brought us to life*
> *using the true Word, showing us off as the crown of all his creatures.*
> James 1:16-18, The Message

Assigned Reading: *The Abba Factor*, Chapter 11

Chapter Summary

Since the Father of Lights is, by nature freely giving and withholding nothing, then our moving from orphans to heirs is not about any change on His side, but our removing the barriers that hinders His cascading grace. He graces us to forgive authorities for misrepresentation of the Father's love; this is the first step to moving from orphan to an heir.

Just like Elijah to Elisha, the Lord is giving us an opportunity to choose natural fathers or supernatural fathers, natural ways or supernatural ways. Seeking forgiveness and restitution from somebody you've wounded opens the passage ways of the Spirit for God to accelerate your transformation. In this relational kingdom it's important to acknowledge our need to be sons and daughters to spiritual fathers and mothers, to open our hearts again to those whom the Lord wants to connect us as family—and thus conduits of His grace.

Because our Father knows WHAT we need and WHEN we need it, living in sonship by the Spirit is being clothed in humility, patience, and the heart for focused listening. Ultimately, it's the Father's voice that changes everything. The Father's voice creates in us will, desire, and energizing power to do His good pleasure (Phil. 2:13, AMP). Sons delight in finishing the Father's unfinished business—and He provides everything (and more) to live the overflowing life.

Sonship is not received by information, education, or even inspiration,
but by the revelation of the Holy Spirit

Questions:

1) Why is it so important to forgive those authorities that have misrepresented Father's love?

2) Why are patience and submission such obvious indicators of sonship?

3) Explain the relationship of cultivating the Presence of God to an ongoing transformation toward sonship:

4) What has the Father spoken to you (by the Spirit within you, by the Scriptures, etc.) that convinces you that you have an inheritance, and that you never have to fear lack?

Sonship is not received by information, education, or even inspiration,
but by the revelation of the Holy Spirit

5) Where do you see yourself right now in the red Mustang convertible?

• •

Supplemental Article

A Sure Inheritance

The inside joke among financial planners and Estate Planning agents goes like this,

"How do you make a small fortune?"
"You inherit a large fortune and spend it down."

The truth is, we live in a culture where material possessions are important, and the matter of leaving an inheritance to one's children is worthy of consideration. An entire industry exists to help people plan for their children's future financial well-being. Most parents give a lot of thought to the issue of inheritance—and it becomes a controlling anxiety among some.

But it's not just a phenomenon of Western Capitalism. If we go back as far as 7,000 years, we see in the earliest record of human civilization a concern for an inheritance. In the Bible we read that "A good man leaves an inheritance to his children's children" (Proverbs 13:22).

Furthermore, God himself is providing an inheritance for His Son—and we are it! (see Ephesians 1:18). All of that to say, inheritances are not to be taken lightly.

However, I am mindful that we live in a world where resources are limited—and often scarce; and that there are many people who don't have the privilege of receiving a large inheritance from their parents. Some have good, well-meaning parents, but not necessarily a significant accumulation of resources to be handed down. Others, tragically, have neglectful parents. Whatever the case may be, the lack of an inheritance can be a source of wounding for a person's soul. Many individuals (especially in current North American society) have carried the scars of rejection or disappointment because his parents failed to leave them an inheritance. Or the inheritance that was left became a source of strife and disintegration within the family, rather than a blessing.

Sonship is not received by information, education, or even inspiration,
but by the revelation of the Holy Spirit

We find such a story in Genesis 27, where Jacob (the deceiver) cheats his brother out of his birthright AND his father's blessing. You can hear the pain in Esau's voice when he *"cried out with an exceedingly great and bitter cry and said to his father, 'Bless me, even me also, O my father!' … 'Have you not reserved a blessing for me?'"* (vv. 34, 36).

Isaac only had ONE blessing to give. Not only had Esau lost his material inheritance; but a spiritual inheritance as well. Heartbreaking!

As I was reading this I sensed Holy Spirit saying to me, "Sometimes you feel like Esau—like your Father only has one blessing to give. But God is not like that! There is no shortage with Him. He delights to give, and He delights to bless ALL of His children. Trust Him. He has all that you need."

The by-line of this book is *"Knowing yourself through your Father's eyes."* I trust that what you have seen and heard here is that the Father doesn't love you because you perform a certain way, possess certain beliefs (right doctrines), or measure up to someone else's standards of what a "good Christian" is. Your Heavenly Father loves you because you are

His, and He loves to be with us in good times and bad. Nothing can separate us from His love (Rom. 8:38-39).

Sons know where they came from and where they are going—the bosom (heart) of the Father. Sons know (by revelation) that they have a Father, that they have a home, they can be themselves, and that they have an inheritance. In other words, sons have nothing to hide, nothing to prove, nothing to fear, and nothing to lose.

I want to encourage you today with these words—if you are a child of God, then you are an heir of God—and that makes you a joint heir with Christ (Romans 8:17, 32). You have a significant inheritance, and you will never lack what you need. God's resources are not limited—the pantry will never be empty for you, and you will never, ever be alone. Not because of how you behave, but because that's who Our Father is.

As long as you keep looking to natural sources, you will be disappointed. Your earthly parents may fail you; but your heavenly Father will never fail you. He is the Good Father, and You can trust Him. Your inheritance, in Him, is sure. Now are we the sons of God, and that changes everything.

Sonship is not received by information, education, or even inspiration,
but by the revelation of the Holy Spirit

Personal Reflection

What is the Lord saying to you?

Congratulations!

You have completed

Here's your invitation to **take the next step** in *The Abba Journey* toward living as a son/daughter who has nothing to hide, nothing to prove, nothing to fear, and nothing to lose.

The Abba Formation, the third part of this trilogy, will reveal the Spirit's role in building your personal transformation. In book 3 we discover the inside-out process of the indwelling Spirit, who searches out the Father's will and purpose for us, then discloses it to our spirit. You will discover how to get full and stay full of the overflowing God himself, and be renewed in your original, unique "genius."

Part 1: *The Abba Foundation: Knowing the Father Through the Eyes of Jesus*, by Chiqui Wood. Burkhart Books, 2018. ISBN: 978-1-940359601

Part 3: *The Abba Formation: The Holy Spirit's Role in Your Personal Transformation*, by Kerry Wood. Burkhart Books, 2018. ISBN: 978-1-940359656.

Also, remember that Jesus told us to "go into all the world and make disciples of all nations" (Matthew 28:19). **Consider inviting two other friends to join you on *The Abba Journey*.** Form a triad and lead them through the journey.

Let's fulfill the Great Commission together!

The *Abba* FORMATION

The Holy Spirit is the personal, generating power of your transformation.

Week 1
Deep Calls to Deep

Meditation Verse

> *Deep calls unto deep at the noise of Your waterfalls;*
> *All Your waves and billows have gone over me. (Psalm 42:7)*

The verse in context:

> *Why are you cast down, O my soul? And why are you disquieted within me? Hope in God, for I shall yet praise Him for the help of His countenance. O my God, my soul is cast down within me; Therefore I will remember You from the land of the Jordan, And from the heights of Hermon, from the Hill Mizar. Deep calls unto deep at the noise of Your waterfalls; All Your waves and billows have gone over me. The LORD will command His lovingkindness in the daytime, And in the night His song shall be with me—A prayer to the God of my life.*
> Psalm 42:5-8

Assigned Reading: *The Abba Formation*, Introduction and Chapter 1

Chapter Summary

The deep things in God calls to the deepest part of you and me. This is deeper than one's emotions; the deepest part of man is spirit (Greek: *pneuma*), not soul (Greek: *psuche*). In Psalms 42, David is dealing with depression, *"Why are you cast down, oh my soul?"* And yet he knows there is a deeper place—a place where the "waterfalls of God" will wash over him. Jesus later describes this as "rivers of living water flowing out of a man's inner most being" (see John 7:38-39). Into this deeper place is where we commune with God and God with us—commanding His lovingkindness while we are awake and singing songs over us, and in us, even while we sleep (Psalm 42:8).

The story of Mephibosheth provides insight into the orphan heart and how the Holy Spirit comes to replace the lies we have believed about God. Mephibosheth is raised in a city of refuge, surrounded by fugitives who disdain the law, and no doubt schooled in lies about David. But David's servant, a type of the Holy Spirit, finds Him, brings him to the palace and introduces him to the King, and begins to acquaint him with his inheritance. Satan uses traumatic experiences in our childhood and life to tell us lies about God (and ourselves), so the Holy Spirit will use divinely-empowered experiences to replace those lies with the Truth.

The Holy Spirit is the personal, generating power of your transformation.

Neither **willpower nor information** are sufficient in and of themselves to replace the lies that we have believed and have little power to bring lasting change. We need the Spirit of God. The demonstration of the Spirit's power is the internal and experiential engine of change.

Questions:

1) In the Introduction the author reviews the importance of understanding the impacts of "the *Abba* cry," introducing a chart that compares characteristics of the *orphan spirit* and a *spirit of sonship*. Why is this significant for our understanding and which of these comparisons spoke the loudest to you?

2) In what ways is Mephibosheth's story all of humanity's story? How do you personally relate to it? What are some lies you've believed about God and yourself?

3) Why isn't willpower and mental discipline (education and therapy) enough to solve our problems or bring lasting transformation?

4) Why did Paul come to Corinth saying (paraphrased), "I don't want to know anything except Jesus Christ and Him crucified. My preaching was not just about persuasive words, but the demonstration of the Spirit's power"?

The Holy Spirit is the personal, generating power of your transformation.

5) From the supplemental reading, why is understanding the difference between soul and spirit important?

• •

Supplemental Article

The Importance of the Trinity of Man

To be able to partner well with the Holy Spirit for our transformation, it is very helpful to understand how and where the Holy Spirit abides in us. Since mankind is made in the image of God, we resemble God in His three-fold nature (the Trinity). As God is Father, Son, and Holy Spirit, mankind is a spirit, possessing a soul (mind, will and emotions), and living in a physical body. The creation account of Genesis describes God's intention, "Let us make man in our image and after our likeness," (Gen. 1:26).

• Man's spirit is part of the spiritual world that connects to God (who is spirit, Jn. 4:24), and communicates with God.
• Man's soul (Greek: *psuche, psyche*), connects us with other living beings through reason, feeling, and emotion.
• Man's body (*soma*) connects man to the physical universe, knowing and experiencing through the five physical senses. These overlap and communicate with one-another.

Notice how Paul's prayer for the Thessalonians reveals this trinitarian dimension of man:

Now may the God of peace Himself sanctify you completely; and may your whole spirit, soul, and body be preserved blameless at the coming of our Lord Jesus Christ.
1 Thess. 5:23

Paul's prayer for these saints to be preserved and "completely" blameless indicates that he is concerned with the total person of each believer. In the second part of the verse he enumerates the three elements that make up the nature of man.

Additional insight as to how these three facets of the human person work and overlap is seen in Hebrews 4:12, "*For the word of God*

The Holy Spirit is the personal, generating power of your transformation.

is living and powerful, and sharper than any two-edged sword, piercing even to the division of soul and spirit, and of joints and marrow, and is a discerner of the thoughts and intents of the heart."

Notice that the soul and spirit, invisible, immaterial parts of man, are distinctly different; the Word (*logos*) of God discerns the distinction between the thoughts of the mind (soul) and motives of the heart (spirit). The metaphor the Hebrew writer gives is significant in that is shows both life-source and overlap. The same way the marrow (in the center) of the bone creates the blood that gives life to the bone and flesh, the spirit of man gives life to the soul and body. Solomon said, "Guard your heart with all diligence, for out of it flows the issues (forces) of life," (Pr 4:23). The same way the marrow produces the blood that then gives life to the body, even so out the spirit of man (heart) life flows to the soul and body.

Finally, we must understand the overlap of the three. The same way the three Persons of the Trinity are both distinct Persons but mutually-indwelling (John 17:21, 23), so the three parts of man all impact each other. If you were to look at a cross-section of a bone you would see that the marrow is yellow, then there is a deep red before the white of the bone—there is an overlap. We know there is an overlap between thoughts of the mind and electrical impulses and chemical secretions of the adrenal system (which converts our intangible thoughts to chemicals in our brain cells). Have you ever walked into a store and heard a song playing on the speaker system that reminds you of some person or experience of your past? The memory system connects the intangible sound with the experience you have stored that is connected emotionally to the song. Suddenly, you find yourself having an emotional experience simply by hearing sounds.

Why is this important? Each of us have had experiences in our life, some of them lovely and some traumatic, which have heart beliefs and mental/emotional responses attached to each of those memories. The same way our most arduous diseases must be treated at a cellular level, our deepest spiritual strongholds and emotional-physical addictions must be treated at the deepest level—the level of the spirit—for real transformation. If this is so, then we can understanding how to connect with God at the deepest level, and learning how to develop our spirit will be very important.

How often have you awakened in the morning with a worship song running through your mind? Psalm 77:6 shows us this is one of the ways God uses our experiences in Him to draw us daily and to invite us into intimate conversation. *"I call to remembrance my song in the night; I meditate within my heart, and my spirit makes diligent search."* If you'll listen for those songs in the night when you first wake up,

---

The Holy Spirit is the personal, generating power of your transformation.

you'll find the gateway of your soul opened to connect to God. Sing the song to Him as you start your day (also see Job 35:10; Ps. 16:7).

••

Personal Reflection

What is the Lord saying to you?

The Holy Spirit is the personal, generating power of your transformation.

The Holy Spirit is the personal, generating power of your transformation.

Week 2
An Inside Job

Meditation Verse

For the Spirit searches all things, yes, the deep things of God. (1 Cor. 2:10)

The verse in context:

> *But as it is written: "Eye has not seen, nor ear heard, Nor have entered into the heart of man the things which God has prepared for those who love Him." But* **God has revealed them to us** *through His Spirit. For the Spirit searches all things, yes,* **the deep things of God**. *For what man knows the things of a man except the spirit of the man which is in him?*
>
> 1 Corinthians 2:9-11

Assigned Reading: *The Abba Formation*, Chapter 2

Chapter Summary

Jesus told His disciples at the Last Supper that He was going to send the Holy Spirit, who would be actively taking everything the Father gives to Jesus and downloading it to those who receive His Spirit (John 16:13, 14). Paul says the same thing in a different way—The Spirit of God goes in and searches out the depths of the Father's purposes for the world and each of His children (1 Cor. 2:10). It is the Spirit's doing, which means our spiritual maturity is not a product of our own efforts; it's an "inside job" in which the Holy Spirit downloads the will and plan of God in our spirits. We must learn to partner with the Spirit.

We have been invited into the ongoing conversation of the Trinity—with both the Spirit and Son sharing with us what the Father is saying about us and about His plans and purposes for our world. He has invited us to enter into the Triune conversation by prayer and worship. The orphan mindset can only look in from a distance—but sons come boldly and join the conversation.

In 1 Corinthians 2 Paul uses the idea of synchronization to explain how the Holy Spirit gets us "up to speed" with God's will and plan. Two illustrations for this *Abba* formation process are the comparing of two halves of an avocado, and the transmission of an automobile (releasing the power of the engine slowly to the rear axle) until one can be synchronized to the other.

The Holy Spirit is the personal, generating power of your transformation.

At the same time, the internal effect of the Spirit is to synchronize believer's spirit, soul, and body into an integrated wholeness so that our being, believing and behaving are one.

Questions:

1) How does the "inside-out" life contrast to the "outside-in" life?

2) Why was Paul so emphatic about not ministering from a place of man's wisdom but by the demonstration of the Spirit?

3) In what way does an avocado (cut in half) illustrate the Spirit's synchronization (*sunkrinō*) between God's heart and our own?

4) In what way does the transmission of a car illustrate how the Holy Spirit works transformation in a believer's life?

The Holy Spirit is the personal, generating power of your transformation.

5) In what way does staying full of the Spirit impact the need to know the will of God or the concern to be in God's will?

6) What other thought stood out to you that you would like to talk about?

• •

Supplemental Article

No Transformation Without This

A prominent Indian pastor, tells the following story in Ravi Zacharias', *Beyond Opinion: Living the Faith We Defend*. It develops slowly, but it's worth it.

In the years immediately following World War II, Abkhazian elder Murat Yagan reflects on a time he spent in eastern Turkey. There he became friends with an elderly couple. Life had been good to them, but their one sadness was that they missed their only son, who had left some years before to work in Istanbul.

One day when Murat visited them, the old couple were bursting with pride, eager to show him the new tea cupboard that their son had just shipped from Istanbul. It was a handsome piece of furniture, and the woman had already arranged her best tea set on its upper shelf. Murat was polite but curious. Why would their son go through such an expense to send them a tea cupboard? And if the purpose of this piece of furniture was storage, why were there no drawers? "Are you sure it's a tea cupboard?" Murat asked. They were sure.

But the question continued to nag at Murat. Finally, just before leaving, he said, "Do you mind if I have a look at this tea cupboard?" With their permission, he turned the backside around and unscrewed a couple of packing boards. A set of cabinet doors swung open to

The Holy Spirit is the personal, generating power of your transformation.

149

reveal a fully operative ham radio set. That "tea cupboard," of course, was intended to connect the couple to their son. But unaware of its real contents, they were simply using it to display their china.

This is how we have been using "the Trinity". It is our theological tea cupboard, upon which we display our finest doctrinal china, our prized assertion that Jesus, a fully human and divine, and the Holy Spirit has come to empower the Church. We are quite sure we understand the Trinity. But, what if, inside the Trinity is concealed a powerful communications tool that could connect us to the rest of reality (visible and invisible), allow us to navigate the many issues of our time? What if, the Trinity (being the very relational nature and essence of God), is the only way to understand the teachings of Jesus and unlock their power, be transformed, and touch our world?

At a time when spiritual imagination and boldness are at an all-time low and the Christian Church seems to totter on the edge of irrelevance, perhaps now is the time to remove the packing board from this tea cupboard and release its contents.

The Bible introduces love as an interpersonal quality requiring a subject-object relationship that originates in and is available as the love of the Father and the Son through the Holy Spirit. This is wholeness, this is "normal," long before creation, and certainly before creation became broken and non-relational. The Father loves the Son before the creation of the world (John 17:24). The infinite personal medium through whom this love is communicated is the Holy Spirit, and He is the one who pours the love of God in our hearts as well (Romans 5:5). There is no wholeness, no transformation, without the dynamic, never-ending love of the Father, Son and Holy Spirit.

It's the Main Thing

Book One of the Abba trilogy, The Abba Foundation, begins with the Trinity as the basis for everything; we underscore it again here. In this relational world, created by a wholly-loving, overflowing, relational God, the psalmist rightly articulates all our worship as pointing toward "the beauty of holiness" (Psalm 29:2 KJV). Wholeness is beautiful. Transformation is beautiful; both qualities require harmony and relatedness. Our gazing on the enthralling being of the Triune God should result in true worship. This is who we are responding to who He is. And that worship, like the tenth leper that returned to worship Jesus, makes us "every wit whole"— transforms us, restores us, puts us back together. Transformation is never an individual quest.

The Christian pursuit of worship has been made a purely individualistic endeavor. Christian disciplines do not appear to be much different from the lonely

The Holy Spirit is the personal, generating power of your transformation.

aspiration of Eastern religions except that Christian words have been inserted. But we are transformed by looking into another's face (2 Cor 3:16)—this is sheer intimacy, not isolation.

The lack of Trinitarian thinking and teaching has exacerbated the prevailing individualism of our culture and has brought it right into our Christian life and practice. If we do not think of God as a relational being in Himself, we can't appreciate the fact that we are made to reflect His Triune image via our relationships with one another. We actually need one another to comprehend the majesty and love of God and respond in true worship as a community (Ephesians 3:14-21).

Do you realize that the Scriptures were written to communities and were read in community until the Guttenberg press? Many of the psalms were written in the plural and some sung, not to God, but to one another (see, for instance, Psalms 95-100; 122-126; 132-144). The Scriptures teach us that when we are discouraged, we are to encourage one another, to lift up one another's feeble hands in adoration to God. The Church prayed together, sang together, studied the Word together and did life together. As we do the same we begin to reflect our interdependence on one another and thereby reflect the being of God in our corporate worship.

Transformation (holiness, wholeness), in the final analysis, is therefore otherward and unselfconscious. As a final note, for example, consider the trinitarian example from John 5:19-27; 16:13, 14. The Father entrusts all things to the Son: his authority, his power over life, and judgment. But the Son will do nothing by himself; He will only do what He sees the Father doing. The Spirit will not speak of Himself nor seek His own glory. He will bring glory to Jesus by taking what belongs to Jesus and showing them to us.

Three self-giving, other-centered Persons constitute the amazing God whom we worship! Their wholeness/holiness is our destiny—we call it transformation. It is this aspect of God's character that we seek to reflect in our life and walk as the Church of Jesus Christ.

The Holy Spirit is the personal, generating power of your transformation.

Personal Reflection

What is the Lord saying to you?

The Holy Spirit is the personal, generating power of your transformation.

152

Week 3
Restored to Childlikeness

Meditation Verse

> *Assuredly, I say to you, unless you are converted [strephō —turn back] and become as little children, you will by no means enter the kingdom of heaven. (Matthew 18:3)*

The verse in context:

> *At that time the disciples came to Jesus, saying, "Who then is greatest in the kingdom of heaven?" Then Jesus called a little child to Him, set him in the midst of them and said, "Assuredly, I say to you, unless you are converted [strephō—turn back] and become as little children, you will by no means enter the kingdom of heaven. Therefore, whoever humbles himself as this little child is the greatest in the kingdom of heaven. Whoever receives one little child like this in My name receives Me.*
>
> Matthew 18:2-5

Assigned Reading: *The Abba Formation*, Chapter 3

Chapter Summary

When we are seeing a thing for the first time, our view is more objective, not tainted by bad experiences. When Jesus tells the crowds they must return (*straphete*) to an original place of childlikeness, he wasn't saying "try hard to humble yourself" but come back to what you are by nature (a trusting child). Children are born innocent, fearless, dependent, not self-conscious, transparent, dreamers, imaginative, energetic, learners, impartial, non-prejudiced, and relational. But being born into a broken world with imperfect parents and siblings, it's not long before hurts, wounds, disappointment, and possibly even abuse get hard-wired into the brain and emotions. We are even taught as children to mistrust others as a result of the world's broken state and our innate childhood genius gets bound and gagged by the wounds of life— the enemy is master at using these experiences as entry points for lies that convince us that we are other than, less than loveable by a holy God.

Childhood characteristics, including but not limited to fearlessness, spontaneity, simple trust, creativity and imagination, are genius traits that the Holy Spirit works to restore in every son and daughter of God. The Holy Spirit teaches us at a deep heart level to cry "Daddy" again.

The Holy Spirit is the personal, generating power of your transformation.

Finally, we discuss how the enemy will even use all of us to "offend one of these little ones." Every time we insult, reject, hurt, or dishonor someone, we play a role in robbing them of the innocence, freedom and fearlessness of childlikeness. The Holy Spirit is working in us to both be restored to childlikeness and become a tool of restoration for others.

Questions:

1) What are some characteristics of childlikeness that we can expect the Holy Spirit to restore in us?

2) When Jesus brought the child to stand as a picture of the way to experience the Kingdom, what was He saying?

3) List some characteristics of childlikeness listed in the chapter and why these might be important for our restoration.

4) Review the list of some of the ways we offend one-another and damage the childlikeness. Do any of them speak to your own history?

5) What is the Bible definition of genius as revealed in 1 Corinthians 2:15-16, and what kind of questions does that raise in you?

6) We've been taught all our lives that the big objective is to "grow up" and put away childishness. What is the difference between childlikeness and childishness, and in what ways can we become childlike again?

• •

Supplemental Article

Read the following poem, not as a wish for escapism, or fleeing responsibility, but as a deep yearning to "return" to what we were created to be. Then reflect on how the Lord might want us to enjoy our days a little more—not take ourselves so seriously—to be sons again.

I Want to Be a Child Again

I want to be a child again …

When it doesn't matter what's right and what's wrong,
When you don't know the words to the song,
When the town that you live in is big as Hong Kong,
And your parents tell you when to just "run along."

I want to be a child again …

To feel like everything's going my way,
To live on the moon for a year and a day,
To run around carefree, with friends, and just play,
And nobody's taking my dreams far away.

I want to be a child again …

I'd look at the world with my rainbow eyes,
I'd read about wonders and not just hear lies,
I'd shake off my shackles and take to the skies,
And eat a dozen blueberry pies!

I want to be a child again …

The Holy Spirit is the personal, generating power of your transformation.

So everything bad would just run down the drain,
So I'd scrape my knee, it gets kissed again,
So nothing I do is for somebody's gain,
And maybe, just maybe, I'd feel whole again.

I want to be a child again

But this time …
I don't want to grow up.

Copyright © Emma Gregory | 2009.

• •

Personal Reflection

What is the Lord saying to you?

Week 4
The Gardener of the Soul

Meditation Verse

> *The Spirit of the Lord is upon me, anointing me to preach*
> *... release ... give ...bind up ... and comfort .... (Luke 4:18-19)*

The verse in context:

> *The Spirit of the Lord is upon me, because He has anointed me*
> *to proclaim good news to the poor. He has sent me to proclaim*
> *liberty [freedom] to the captives and recovering of sight to the*
> *blind, to set at liberty those who are oppressed to proclaim the*
> *acceptable year of the Lord's favor.*
>
> Luke 4:18-19, ESV

Assigned Reading: *The Abba Formation*, Chapter 4

Chapter Summary

Our soul is like a garden that can have both beautiful flowers and weeds growing up together. The Holy Spirit is the gardener, fully committed to lovingly cultivate our souls into a place of beauty and a reflection of God's glory and redemption.

There are at least four ways the Holy Spirit works in us via the *Abba* cry (recalibrating our believing and thinking by releasing God's thoughts deep within us); displacing a slave-mindset, reformatting with a sonship mentality, activating a daily partnership with the Father, and restoring childlike characteristics in us at the deepest levels.

Because God is a relational being, He does life as partnership. We listed numerous ways to partner with the Holy Spirit.

We explore "the Joy Ride" as a prophetic picture and asked which of the seats in the red convertible are we sitting in, that is, what is the condition of the soil of our souls?

The Holy Spirit is the personal, generating power of your transformation.

Questions:

1) What was Jesus's understanding of what the Holy Spirit was doing in and through His ministry (Isa. 61; Luke 4:18-19)?

2) Which of the four works of the *Abba* cry speaks to you the most?

3) Look at the list of ways to partner with the Holy Spirit. Which of those would you want to discuss further?

4) How's your heart? What do you sense the Spirit is working on right now?

5) Of the seats in the red convertible Mustang story, which "condition" do you find most similar to where you are now and why?

The Holy Spirit is the personal, generating power of your transformation.

6) After reading the Supplemental Reading, think about ways we (adults) may not be listening to the father's voice as well as we think. How can child-likeness change this?

• •

Supplemental Article

Children Are Better Listeners

Who among you will listen to this or pay close attention in times to come?

Isa. 42:23

Jesus often prefaces His teaching with "Listen Close!" Well, that's my paraphrase; the Scriptures would say, "Verily, verily," or "Let him that has ears, hear!" He certainly understood the connection between dullness of heart and dullness of hearing (see Is. 6:10). When we talk about the gardening of the soul, one of the primary areas the Spirit must work on is our willingness and attentiveness in listening—hearing His voice.

In the light of what you have read regarding the genius characteristics of early childhood, and Jesus' admonition that we must "return" to our original child-likeness, would it surprise you that totally unrelated research shows that *listening well* and *childhood genius* follow an identical path?

What do you suppose would be the toughest age group to get to sit still and listen? If you've ever taught fifth grade boys at church (in what we used to call Sunday School), or first graders on any occasion, you might think one of those would be a slam dunk answer.

In *"The Plateau Effect"*[6] Sullivan and Thompson reference Ralph Nichols, professor of rhetoric at the University of Minnesota, who is considered the father of research on listening. He devised a simple test. He enlisted school teachers of all grade levels in Minnesota to stop what they were doing in mid-class and ask kids to describe what the teachers

---

[9]Bob Sullivan and Hugh Thompson. *The Plateau Effect: Getting from Stuck to Success*. Dutton, a Member of Penguin Group (USA), Inc:. Excerpted with permission from the publisher. © 2013.

were talking about. **He discovered that the youngest children are the best listeners**. On tests to measure how well people pay attention, the first-graders gave a correct answer 90% of the time.

By junior high, correct answers drop to 44%. In high school, scores plummet to 25%. It gets worse! When a 10-minute oral presentation is given to adults, 75% can't even recall the subject just 24 hours later. Does this sound familiar?

You've heard it said that the older we get, the more information our minds store, and "the filing cabinets get full". In addition, Nichols says, our accumulated knowledge causes us to "skim" information. Most don't read deeply and no longer listen carefully. Adults have a storehouse of experiences and stories they want to tell, so rather than listening well, we are busy thinking about what we are going to say as soon as the other person will take a breath! Children, on the other hand, have no hardened preconceptions, and, as a result, soak everything in.

Likewise, the older we get, the more we feel we've got God pretty well figured out. That would be a good thing if our understanding of God weren't so "grown up." Unfortunately, the same way we overestimate our listening skills, we overestimate our clarity on knowing God. It means we're more likely to "skim" God's Word, to "fast forward" our times with God and the opportunities to hear His voice. Without realizing it, we only hear what already matches (reinforces) our theological position. Repeatedly, Jesus would quiz His disciples after His teaching—and often His response was, "How is it that after hearing you don't understand these things," (Mark 8:17-19)?

What does this have to do with the Holy Spirit's work to restore us to childlikeness?

It is the Holy Spirit that gives us the ears of a child to hear again—to soak up the Father's voice as though we had never heard it before. It is the Holy Spirit that causes words to leap off the page enabling us to see something and hear something in a new way. The Holy Spirit alone can deliver us from a spirit of dullness, Isaiah's dreadful description, "Having eyes, they can't see, and having ears, they can't hear." It is the Holy Spirit who unshackles us from so many stories we've been rehearsing of our past that we can't see new stories for our future.

Humanly speaking, paying attention to God doesn't get easier as we age; it is actually more difficult. The same way our child genius gets snuffed out with slander and fear, our hearing grows dull with accumulation of experiences and "conventional wisdom". It becomes more difficult to avoid leaning to our own understanding. But He wants us to be curious again, creative again, daring again, and awestruck again.

"Listen to My voice again," He says. "Come to me openly like a child. Don't you think I have some

The Holy Spirit is the personal, generating power of your transformation.

new things to tell you? Behold (look and listen!), I do a new thing—I have a lot more to tell you, things you never knew existed. This isn't a variation on the same old thing. This is new, brand-new, something you'd never guess or dream up. When you hear this you won't be

able to say, 'I knew that all along'" (Isa. 43:19, The Message).

For faith comes from hearing, and (this kind of spiritual) hearing through the word (rhema) of Christ.
Romans 8:17

• •

Personal Reflection

What is the Lord saying to you?

The Holy Spirit is the personal, generating power of your transformation.

161

The Holy Spirit is the personal, generating power of your transformation.

Week 5

The Language of Sonship

Meditation Verse

*It is the Spirit who gives life; the flesh profits nothing.
The words that I speak to you are spirit,
and they are life. (John 6:63)*

The verse in context:

> *Does this throw you completely? What would happen if you saw the
> Son of Man ascending to where he came from? The Spirit can make life.
> Sheer muscle and willpower don't make anything happen. Every word
> I've spoken to you is a Spirit-word, and so it is life-making. But some of
> you are resisting, refusing to have any part in this.*
>
> John 6:61-63

Assigned Reading: *The Abba Formation*, Chapter 5

Chapter Summary

One could presume that if God created the heavens and earth with His
words, calls His Son The Word, and upholds and sustains everything He has
made with His word, then language would be an important theme in God's plan
of redemption of that creation. Language shapes how people think, construct
reality, and is significant in forming culture (see the Supplemental Reading).
Thus Sonship has its own language—a language of royalty and honor, which
is nothing less than being invited into the ongoing conversation of the Trinity.

Being made in God's image means sharing life at the level of language,
which is an inside out life. Sonship communicates in the language of
abundance. But in sonship, the language of abundance is about what you've
already received by virtue of being in Christ, not what you're trying to obtain.

Sonship speaks the language of affirmation, a primary characteristic of the
Triune conversation. The language of affirmation is how we encourage one
another in the smaller steps of day-to-day obedience and living. Criticism is a
foreign language in the kingdom of love.

Sonship communicates in the language of the supernatural: Spirit to
spirit. Jesus is first introduced by His cousin, John, as the baptizer in the Holy
Spirit—the initiator of the language of the Spirit. Additional recommended
reading and a fairly thorough biblical survey of spiritual language is provided.

The Holy Spirit is the personal, generating power of your transformation.

Negative experiences or stories about the language of the Spirit are never enough evidence to trump the biblical foundations and priority of Jesus' heavenly ministry. Spiritual language is so important to our transformation that the Church is born in the experience, and our development is continually enhanced by it (Acts 2:1-4).

Questions:

1) What are the three "in your face" evidences that show us the importance of words to our very life and freedom?

2) What is the *language of honor*, and where does it come from?

3) What is the *language of abundance*, and how is it different from our carnal notions of getting rich?

4) What is the *language of affirmation*, and how is it different from the language of honor?

The Holy Spirit is the personal, generating power of your transformation.

5) What are the three biblical anchors that establish the *language of the Spirit* as normative for the New Testament Church?

6) What questions does this raise for you about how the Spirit shapes the culture of the Church as the colony of Heaven? Any other questions?

• •

Supplemental Article

Language as a Transforming Agent

Different languages consist of a variety of differing vocabulary and differing structures. By language, I can place a thought that is in my mind, into your mind, transcending time and space. Something Abraham Lincoln said in Gettysburg 150 years ago can shape my mind today though language transmitted by print. Our sounds, using air and vibration (from our vocal chords) move through the air, creating a vibration on the human ear drum, which the brain takes and translates into words, which are associated with thoughts, translated to meaning, (events, concepts, actions, etc.).

God has given complex language uniquely to humans (and angels), and uses language to impart His ideas (and ways) into our minds and hearts—transcending time and space. Language is one reason different cultures pay attention to different facts or ideas. Is it true that speakers of different cultures attend to the world differently? Does language really guide what we see? Does it blind us to certain other realities that our culture deems unimportant?

Charlemagne, Holy Roman Emperor said, "To have a second language is to have a second soul." This speaks to the depth of our knowing and being human and how it is communicated to others, and to the intrinsic power of language to shape us.

Frederick the Great of Prussia said, "I speak English to my

The Holy Spirit is the personal, generating power of your transformation.

accountants, French to my ambassadors, Italian to my mistress, Latin to my God, and German to my horse." This hints that the strengths (or focus) of certain cultures are articulated most precisely through that language. For example, the Corinthians, known for their immorality had literally hundreds of words or phrases for sexual intercourse (this speaks to their well-known perversion and preoccupation with sex). The Navajo Indians have dozens of verbs that describe ways of eating and drinking. Can you imagine the most frequent concept in American English? It's various descriptions of time. We are time-conscious—"time is money." The point is, our language is not only shaped by our experience, but shapes the thinking of future generations.

Cognitive scientist, Lera Boroditsky, has done ground-breaking research on how language shapes our reality.[10] I am drawing heavily from her talks for this article. She observes that some languages are written from left to right, some from right to left, some from top to bottom. Some languages don't have exact numbers or quantities, (which, as you can imagine, has a staggering impact upon that culture's ability to survive in a modern world of mathematics, calculations, computers, science, aerospace, etc).

Languages differ in describing time, directions, colors … some languages don't have a general word for "blue", but words that describe each distinct shade. While Western world thinkers will point forward to speak of the future, and behind them to refer to the past, a certain sub-group of Chileans will point forward to the past (because it is what they can see) and behind them to the future (because they haven't been there yet and can't see it).

Why do I think the way I do? How could I think differently? What thoughts do I wish to think? Which ones do I think are impossible because my culture doesn't have a word (concept) for it? What seems impossible to me simply because my culture has never seen it and thus has no word for it? Which brings us to a more important question—if language shapes our thinking and behavior, would God's restoration strategy include expanding our language?

Wouldn't a God, coming from a limitless world of eternity—without the limits of time or space—have words for things I don't know exists? What if God's language has no sense of impossibility to it? What if when He says something, it is as good as done (in reality, not "as a good as", but it is done)? What if, because He is the "I AM", His language doesn't contain past tense or future tense, but everything is in the NOW, the I AM tense? What if, in His world, one speaks of things that be not as though they were, because there is no such thing as "be not"? What if God's words are not to get

The Holy Spirit is the personal, generating power of your transformation.

166

us to DO something, but to BE someone? What if God's words aren't to give you information, but to give you life? What if, because God is LIFE, every word He speaks is life-giving and creates the reality of what the word describes? What if God never speaks to us simply to answer a question, provide more information, or give direction, but to create the reality of His will and desire in us? And what if you and I were invited into this conversation so that we would, by it, be permanently changed?

What does it mean then to hear Jesus say, "Abide and Me, and let My words abide in you—then you will ask whatever you will and it will be done to you." What does Jesus mean when He says, "My words, they are spirit and they are life" (John 6:63)? Wouldn't it be cool if He could speak His language in us—beyond the limits of our mind, (with all its cultural limitations)—but in our eternally configured spirit, so that what He is saying "becomes" reality in us? What if God were to make a spiritual language available to us—a language not having the restrictions or limitations of a temporal world, or even of the human mind? Would we be transformed? Of course, He does. This is the Language of Sonship—where Jesus says, the Holy Spirit will take those things of Mine, and reveal them to you (John 16:15).

---

[10]Lisa Boroditsky. "How Language Shapes the Way We Think," https://www.youtube.com/watch?v=RKK7wGAYP6k.

• •

Personal Reflection

What is the Lord saying to you?

The Holy Spirit is the personal, generating power of your transformation.

The Holy Spirit is the personal, generating power of your transformation.

Week 6

The "Active Ingredient" for Transformation

Meditation Verse

> *We ... are being transformed into the same image from glory to glory, just as by the Spirit of the Lord.*
> *(2 Corinthians 3:18)*

The verse in context:

> *Nevertheless when one turns to the Lord, the veil (that covers the ability to see) is taken away. Now the Lord is the Spirit; and where the Spirit of the Lord is, there is liberty. But we all, with unveiled face, beholding as in a mirror the glory of the Lord, are being transformed into the same image from glory to glory, just as by the Spirit of the Lord.*
>
> 2 Cor. 3:16-18

Assigned Reading: *The Abba Formation*, Chapter 6

Chapter Summary

Scripture clearly teaches that the Holy Spirit, not merely church attendance, accountability groups, or new habits, is the active ingredient in our personal transformation. This would mean that attendance to and partnership with the person of the Holy Spirit is paramount. Transformation involves a partnership in which we cooperate with the internal work of the Holy Spirit in our lives. We cooperate by praying it out, playing it out, and saying it out.

The Holy Spirit's mission is to bear witness of our sonship, lead and guide us into all truth (including what's true about ourselves and others} and fill us with power. The Holy Spirit synchronizes our spirits with God's heart, plans, and purposes. The necessary partnership for such synchronization is aided through spiritual language.

The beauty of spiritual language is that it is available to every believer at all times, which means transformation is a priority to the Holy Spirit. The beauty of spiritual language is that it is a physical, tangible witness that God lives inside of every believer by the Spirit. The beauty of spiritual language is that it increases our love for others because the Holy Spirit fills and overflows our inner being with the love of God. The transformation of every believer is the

---

The Holy Spirit is the personal, generating power of your transformation.

work and priority of the indwelling Spirit to bring us to Christlikeness. Our part of the transformation is manifold—articulated in this chapter as praying it out (daily disciplines), playing it out (daily engagement in the mission), and saying it out (the *Abba* cry of prayer and spiritual language).

Questions:

1) What have been some of your preconceived notions of the Holy Spirit? Law-enforcer? KGB informant? Distant and unknowable? Other? Please explain.

2) Why is it important to be a disciple of Jesus rather than a disciple of a disciple of Jesus? And what does the difference look like?

3) Think about the difference between trying to serve the Lord if His presence only resides in a box in Jerusalem, or behind a curtain in the Temple, or even down at the building of your local church, versus having Him in you everywhere you go. List some advantages or disadvantages.

4) Which of the six aspects of the beauty of spiritual language seem most important to you?

The Holy Spirit is the personal, generating power of your transformation.

5) Read James 3:3-6 about the power of the tongue (our words). How does the idea of the "tongue as the most powerful member" inform us as to why the Holy Spirit uses language as a key to transformation and why spiritual language is often misunderstood?

●●●

Supplemental Article

God's Spirit-People

No biblical writer is as clear as the Apostle Paul with regard to the impacts of being God's Spirit-people. Those who have received Christ are both "in Christ" and "in the Spirit." The difference, to Paul, between believers and non-believers, is that non-believers don't have the Holy Spirit in them, believers do have the Holy Spirit in them. To Paul, there are three kinds of people:

Three kinds of people:

1. Spirit-People (*pneumatikoi*) —S/spiritual, having the Spirit in their spirit and living by the understanding and synchronization that the Spirit provides; living out the new identity provided by Christ's gracious gift via the cross; which results in a growing awareness of sonship.

2. Carnal People (*sarkikoi*) —To be "carnal" is most simply

"being ruled by the flesh and the mind". Carnal believers have the Spirit (born again) but do not live by the understanding of the Spirit. They might attend church but mostly live as if they don't have the Spirit (see 1 Cor. 3:1-4). They do not experience what it is to be synchronized with God's thoughts and plans by the Spirit to experience and enjoy the new kingdom life of sons. Believers who are acting as if they are not equipped to walk with God.

3. Natural (non-Spirit) People (*psuchikoi*)—Non-believers, not having the Spirit, not capable of hearing or knowing God because the Spirit, who knows God, is not in them. Thus the things of God are foolishness to them (1 Cor. 2:14). They live in the limits of the mind (psyche) because the life of God is not in them (Eph. 4:18). Paul says, because the Spirit is not in them they cannot accept the things of

The Holy Spirit is the personal, generating power of your transformation.

the Spirit, cannot understand the things of the Spirit, and reject the things of the Spirit—it is foolishness to them (1 Cor. 2:14).

This idea of *psuche-centered* (soulish) people is of particular interest in the light of the Church's fascination with all things psychological. Much of our church-life (and leadership principles) is now psychologically driven, more than Spirit-driven.

To have the Spirit, in Paul's mind, means that this Spirit-people are part of the coming age, the glorious end (*eschaton*), that has already begun—for in Christ old things have passed away and all things have been made new (1 Cor. 5:17). The Holy Spirit is bringing the future age into the here and now, not waiting for us to get there. The Kingdom (rule and reign of God) has come with the outpouring of the Spirit upon the Church. But many are still living as though slaves instead of sons, distant from God instead of reconciled to Him, keeping rules instead of living Life, trying to be "right" instead of rightly-related, performance-driven instead of Presence-dependent. It is the Holy Spirit, sent to the Church by Jesus Himself, who is persistently transforming us into the image of the Son. The Holy Spirit is preparing us for what God has beforehand prepared FOR us in Christ. To Paul, to ignore the Presence of the indwelling Spirit is to live AS IF Jesus hadn't come and the usurping powers and principalities are still in control. Partnership with the Spirit is how the Spirit-people live the life of the age-to-come now.

• •

Personal Reflection

What is the Lord saying to you?

The Holy Spirit is the personal, generating power of your transformation.

Week 7
The Benefits of Praying in the Spirit

Meditation Verse

I pray ... that He [the Father] would grant you, according to the riches of His glory, to be strengthened with might through His Spirit in the inner man. (Ephesians 3:16)

The verse in context:

For this reason I bow my knees to the Father of our Lord Jesus Christ, from whom the whole family in heaven and earth is named, that He would grant you, according to the riches of His glory, to be strengthened with might through His Spirit in the inner man, that Christ may dwell in your hearts through faith; that you, being rooted and grounded in love.

Ephesians 3:14-16

Assigned Reading: *The Abba Formation*, Chapter 7

Chapter Summary

Praying in the S/spirit (my spirit by the Holy Spirit) enables us to participate at a preconceptual (a spiritual knowing that is before cognitive language) level in the conversation of the Trinity. Believers must come to grips with the reality that, as spirit beings, we are designed to know first in our spirits. This is an eternal knowing that is not first processed in the brain but in the heart/spirit. As soon as we put human language to this spirit-knowing, limitless thoughts from a limitless world are squeezed (and distorted) into limited human thought.

Spiritual language enables communication with God, who is a Spirit (John 4:24), that bypasses the limits of our mind. We can communicate with God, the deep things of God—and initially our understanding is "unfruitful". Our mind has to catch up to what our heart already knows. Spiritual Language enables you to pray accurately, according to God's will. The impacts of spiritual language upon the dynamic of effective prayer (praying according to the will of God) cannot be underestimated or over-stated.

Praying in the Spirit—our spirit praying by the Holy Spirit—is how the Holy Spirit synchronizes our hearts to what is in the Father's heart. It is a primary way that God downloads His will and purposes for your life into your "knower", which means grasping and walking in the will of God is not nearly as difficult as we've made it. It's by the Spirit.

The Holy Spirit is the personal, generating power of your transformation.

Praying in the S/spirit provides supernatural rest and strengthens us at the deepest place of our being with every kind of strength we need. This means it also promotes psychological wholeness and resistance to depression. Praying in the S/spirit not only helps a person locate his/her spirit (as distinct from the soul) but releases a spirit of faith as we learn to connect our hearts with our words. Praying in the S/spirit enriches the believer with rivers of revelation, communication, and demonstration (the nine gifts of the Spirit, 1 Cor. 12), and increases our love for others so that the gifts are used in the right way.

Questions:

1) Of the ten benefits of spiritual language listed, which one would be the greatest help to your walk with the Lord and to your effectiveness in helping others?

2) What has been your own exposure to spiritual (prayer) language?

3) Why is prayer language (which bypasses the limits of the mind) such a critical facet of communion with God and confirmation of sonship?

4) How does prayer from your spirit (by the Holy Spirit) promote psychological wholeness and resistance to depression?

5) From the supplemental reading, which one of the four "deep things" of the Father's thoughts toward you seem to be the most needful/helpful to you?

6) If these benefits, and the deep things of the Father, are available to us by the Holy Spirit praying through us, what would be the spiritually-logical corresponding discipline?

••
Supplemental Article

The Deep Things of God

In this chapter we are looking at Paul's insights into how to access the deep things of God that have been made available to every believer by the Holy Spirit. Particularly, in 1 Corinthians, chapter 2, Paul is providing a loving corrective by contrasting different kinds of wisdom—which was a fascination to the Greek mind and culture of Corinth. First, he distinguishes between natural human wisdom (1 Cor. 2:5-6) and godly wisdom (1 Cor. 2:7). Our minds would harken to James' letter that says man's wisdom is "earthly, sensual, and devilish", and God's wisdom is "first pure, then peaceable, easily entreated, full of mercy and good fruits, and without partiality or hypocrisy (James 3:15).

Paul wrote to remind the Corinthians that when he came to them he did not use "the enticing words of man's wisdom" but He spoke words of the Holy Spirit, his preaching confirmed by the demonstration of the Spirit's power (1 Cor. 2:4). And

The Holy Spirit is the personal, generating power of your transformation.

175

why was this partnership with the Spirit so important to Paul and his hearers? He says in his own words, "so that your faith should not be in the wisdom of men but in the power of God" (1 Cor. 2:5).

Unfortunately, many in the Church today still esteem the wisdom of man, intellect, techniques, education, data, metrics, and ingenuity over the wisdom of God. The results is that the Church places its faith in intellect, education, and ingenuity over the presence and power of God. Seminaries are just as busy teaching Greek and Hebrew as ever, and their churches espousing cerebral approaches to preaching, but discount the realities of the seeing, hearing, and knowing in the Spirit.

Paul says that we cannot know the deep things of God by our minds, but by the Holy Spirit who teaches us "the deep things of God" by the revelation of the Spirit (1 Cor. 2:10-11). "No one knows the things of God except the Spirit of God." It is the Holy Spirit, the third member of the Trinity, who through mutually indwelling, unending, loving fellowship with the Father and the Son, discovers (in joyful conversation no doubt) the deep plans and purposes of the Father for each and every one of His children.

By the way, if you think have any lingering thoughts in the back of your mind that God is not totally awestruck-in-love with you, and that perhaps He is out to smack you for some mistake you've made or fed up with your lack of spiritual fervor, you are likely to be much less interested in the deep things of God for you. In some ways (IF God is angry and judgmental) you might subconsciously hope the deep things of God don't ever surface, as if He were actually storing up those things He said He had cast into the "sea of forgetfulness". No, those things aren't o the table any more. His millions of thoughts toward you are good—wholly good (Jer. 29:11).

So what are the "deep things of God" which He is revealing?

1. He is revealing the grand scheme of His love—the redeeming of the nations and gathering all things together in one New Man—Jesus. This is the thought that enraptured Paul to a spontaneous eruption of praise as He was disclosing to the Romans how God has worked drawing both the Jews and Gentiles into one family saying, "Oh the judgments, and His ways past finding out! (Rom. 11:33). The Holy Spirit communicates to us a sense of the grand scope of our redemption—that we belong in the "family of heaven and earth"—and a deep-seated peace about the big questions of "why am I here" and "where am I going?"

2. He is revealing everything that is ours as an inheritance in Christ. Paul says, "… that we might know the things that have been freely given to us by God" (1

The Holy Spirit is the personal, generating power of your transformation.

176

Cor. 2:12). These include "every spiritual blessing in the heavenly places in Christ (Eph. 1:3)—but these are not "spiritual blessings" in the sense of "too heavenly to be any earthly good." These include everything that is included in our salvation (*shalom or sozo*)—healing, deliverance, peace of mind, every earthly blessing as well. In other words, the Holy Spirit is searching out every blessing God has planned for you, and He works to convince that it is yours and to pull you into it.

3. He is revealing "partnership information" for exploits—situations, people, needs, that are all around you so a "divine intervention" can be released on His behalf. Our Triune God does everything relationally, and He wants His sons and daughters to experience the joy of partnership! Later in this same letter Paul says the Holy Spirit gives "gifts," supernatural endowments as the need requires so that others can come to experience the overflowing love of the Father (1 Cor. 12:7-12).

4. The deep things include intimate conversation between Father and sons. In introducing the Holy Spirit to His disciples, Jesus said, "I am going to send you the Holy Spirit … He will guide you into all truth (John 16:13), and He will bring all things to your remembrance that I have said to you" (John 14:26). This is also how His prayer that same night would be answered for every generation to come, "Father make them to know that the same way I am in You, and You are in Me (the intimacy of mutual indwelling), so We are in them … and that (they know) You love them just as You have loved Me" (John 17:21-23).

The deep things of God are the currency of a kingdom that is out of this world. But God rarely discloses His secrets to casual seekers. The deep things of God are worth pursuing as hidden treasure. The one who is sensitive to the Spirit and listening for His voice; the spiritual man or woman whose life is guided and directed by the Spirit and receiving downloads Spirit to spirit, is the man or woman who "has access to everything God's Spirit is doing, but can't be judged by unspiritual critics" (1 Cor. 2:15, The Message).

The Holy Spirit is the personal, generating power of your transformation.

Personal Reflection

What is the Lord saying to you?

The Holy Spirit is the personal, generating power of your transformation.

178

Week 8
Impact of Sonship on Prayer

Meditation Verse

> *Likewise the Spirit also helps in our weaknesses. For we do not know what we should pray for as we ought, but the Spirit Himself makes intercession for us with groanings which cannot be uttered. (Romans 8:26)*

The verse in context:

> *Likewise the Spirit also helps in our weaknesses. For we do not know what we should pray for as we ought, but the Spirit Himself makes intercession for us with groanings which cannot be uttered. Now He who searches the hearts knows what the mind of the Spirit is, because He makes intercession for the saints according to the will of God. And we know that all things work together for good to those who love God, to those who are called according to His purpose … to be conformed to the image of His Son, that He might be the firstborn among many brethren.*
>
> Romans 8:26-29

Assigned Reading: *The Abba Formation*, Chapter 8

Chapter Summary

The orphan spirit (mindset) doesn't have a revelation of Father and home, so prayer is always about convincing, coercing, sacrificing, or earning (e.g. the British petitioner at the beginning of the chapter). But prayer is never about twisting God's arm or overcoming some reluctance on His part. Sons have a revelation that Father is anything but reluctant. It is not making demands upon God but listening, partnering, and asking, "Father, what do You want me to ask You for?" Prayer is also much more than getting something from God. Prayer is a two-way conversation. Jesus teaches us to worship (intimacy) before asking the Father (see "The Lord's Prayer").

Prayer is a trinitarian conversation—We come boldly to the Father (John 16:23), through Jesus Christ (Rom. 5:2), by the Holy Spirit (Rom. 8:26). A spirit of sonship (the work of the Spirit) transforms our desire to pray, makes us bold to enter the Father's presence without shame or timidity, and synchronizes us with the Father's agenda. The Holy Spirit helps us find and sustain a relational rhythm of rest that makes prayer a communion of intimacy rather than drudgery

---

The Holy Spirit is the personal, generating power of your transformation.

or duty. The results of this relational rhythm of rest is an overflowing fullness of thanksgiving and joy.

Paul understood an unbreakable bond between the Spirit's role in prayer and the impacts of a revelation of sonship, specifically by the *Abba* cry. Spiritual orphans lack assurance of Father's care thus their prayer is often reduced to petitioning for their own needs. Sons live in a revelation of the Father's abundance and care. If I know I will never lack, my prayers turn from my own self-preservation to the Father's unfinished business—to the blessing of others—"Ask of Me and I will give you the nations for an inheritance and the ends of the earth for your possession" (Ps. 2:8).

Questions:

1) After seeing Paul's emphasis on prayer as a key means for spiritual maturity, what might this say about cultivating a life of communion with God vs. "putting in your time" in prayer?

2) What are some of the reasons that believers don't pray?

3) In your own words, what is the impact of a revelation of one's sonship on prayer as partnership with God and prayer as intimacy?

The Holy Spirit is the personal, generating power of your transformation.

4) Which of the contrasts between orphans' and sons' prayer spoke to you most clearly? Why?

5) What did you sense the Lord saying to you about your own current experience in prayer?

• •

Supplemental Article

Holy Spirit's Work in Prayer

One of the most transformational books of my life is entitled, *Prayer: Invading the Impossible*, by one of my primary spiritual mentors, Pastor Jack Hayford.[11] In an insightful study in the book, the author traces the Greek word used for "intercession" (ἔντευξις [/ent•yook•sis/]) back to the Hebrew word "*pagah*," and sheds light on how the Holy Spirit works in a believer to partner with the Father's will and purpose. In the context of the Hebrew "*pagah*" the New Testament usage could carry the following applications in our lives:

1. To fall in with, meet with, an interview, a visit,
2. To light upon as if by chance,
3. To fall upon in order to carry out the will of the king, and
4. To press out to predetermined boundaries.

For sake of brevity please consider the work of the Holy Spirit as the activator of your prayer life in your in the last of these four—"pressing out to predetermined boundaries."

[11]Jack Hayford. Prayer is Invading the Impossible. North Brunswick, NJ: Bridge-Logos Pub., 1977.

[12]"pagah" The Greek-English Lexicon of the New Testament (BDAG), 3rd ed.

The Holy Spirit is the personal, generating power of your transformation.

In Joshua, chapters 13-19, following the return of the ten spies who had made detailed maps of the "promised lands", including the reports of giants and abundance in the land, Joshua gathers the heads of the Tribes of Israel. They are meeting with Eleazar the priest "at Shiloh in the presence of the Lord at the entrance to the Tent of Meeting," to apportion to each their allotted inheritance of the Promised Land.

This apportioning process uses the Hebrew word "*Pagah*," which means to reach unto, to intercede, to press unto predetermined boundaries.[9] Imagine Joshua gathering these leaders around a roughly drawn map and, with his finger moving across the map, he begins to assign huge territories to each tribe.

Interestingly, the descriptions of the apportioned lands is not only given by its borders—where the boundaries extend by physical geographical description, but by the number of cities and their villages within each territory. Some territories had as few as six cities and others had twenty or more cities and their surrounding villages. Joshua might have sounded something like this, "Judah, your territory moves from that river which bounds the East of the valley, all the way across the top of that ridge, and back down to the base of the gorge. That's about 800 square miles." Then he continued to map out territory for each tribe. But when he was done he looked at each leader with somber tone and said, "Now you remember what Moses said—'everywhere we set the sole of our foot, the land is ours.' But we know there are giants in the hills, there are armies large and small, there are wild beasts, and there is a lot of land to clear. You will have to push the enemy out, conquer the wild animals, and tame the land—but you are well able!"

This picture of a territory that is given, yet not fully possessed, serves as a metaphor of the indwelling Holy Spirit coaching each believer on his inheritance in Christ. "The territory is yours, but you have to press out to the predetermined boundaries" the Spirit witnesses in our spirit.

Could this scene be what Jesus has in mind when he tells the story of the stewards/managers who invest *minas* (money) and yield a variety of returns to their owner (Luke 19:15-20). Jesus says, "Well done! Because you have been trustworthy in a very small matter (your 1 mina has earned 10 more) take charge of 10 cities." Those cities and villages represent clusters of people, the Lord's inheritance.

Perhaps we have been tempted to see this story as the rewards we will receive in heaven on Judgment Day. But consider that Jesus is talking about the things of the kingdom—light breaking into darkness and retaking what the enemy has stolen. In the personal sense of the Holy Spirit's interceding through us, consider that just as

The Holy Spirit is the personal, generating power of your transformation.

182

the 12 tribes did not receive larger or smaller inheritance on the basis of merit, but by the casting of lots for God's choosing, each tribe had to "press unto those boundaries" by conquering the cities and its inhabitants.

The work of the Holy Spirit, igniting the "*Abba* cry" in the hearts of His children by intercessory prayer, not only gives us spiritual eyes to see what God has apportioned to us as inheritance, but helps us to press into the real life experiencing of all that Jesus paid for by His death, burial, and resurrection. It's never just about stuff, money, titles, achievements, degrees. It is everything represented in the idea of *Shalom* (Hebrew) or *Sozo* (Greek)—healing, soundness, wholeness, salvation, peace of mind—all of this is within our boundaries. Now we must partner with the Spirit to lay hold of it as sons. Jesus says if we set our priority on the Kingdom of God all these "things" will be added as a matter of course—thrown in on top (Matt. 6:33). The Old Testament metaphor of cities and villages represent our inheritance—peoples that we impact for the Kingdom of God.

If you are faithful with little (mammon, money) I will give you true riches (the souls of men).

The Holy Spirit is making you whole to dream again, in innocence, fearlessness, boldness, visions of goodness for the sake of the cities and villages of yet-to-be reached people. The Holy Spirit is in you right now, stirring your heart to rise up and lay hold of everything that Jesus provided for you with His own blood.

· ·

Personal Reflection

What is the Lord saying to you?

The Holy Spirit is the personal, generating power of your transformation.

The Holy Spirit is the personal, generating power of your transformation.

Week 9
On Mission with Triune God

Meditation Verse

And I have declared to them Your name, and will declare it, that the love with which You loved Me may be in them, and I in them (John 17:26)

The verse in context:

> *I do not pray for these alone, but also for those who will believe in Me through their word; that they all may be one, as You, Father, are in Me, and I in You; that they also may be one in Us, that the world may believe that You sent Me. And the glory which You gave Me I have given them, that they may be one just as We are one: I in them, and You in Me; that they may be made perfect in one, and that the world may know that You have sent Me, and have loved them as You have loved Me ... O righteous Father! The world has not known You, but I have known You; and these have known that You sent Me. And I have declared to them Your name, and will declare it, that the love with which You loved Me may be in them, and I in them.*
>
> John 17:20-26

Assigned Reading: *The Abba Formation*, Chapter 9

Chapter Summary

God has given every believer a brand new identity in Christ. Unfortunately, many believers are still "DUI"—driving under the influence of an orphan identity which has them chasing accomplishments to prove who they are or medicating the pain from the past. The grand cost is that the whole earth is groaning, waiting for the manifestation of sons. The groaning is the yearning to see an orphan world restored to Father's house; to finish the Father's business.

God has given us His Spirit, not just to get us to Heaven, but to get us on His mission for humanity. We have talked about the Father's mission to redeem mankind and all of creation. In this sense the Father is the first to send a missionary into the world and both the Son and Spirit are the "sent ones."

The Son's mission is both to finish the Father's unfinished business and to make His name known. We cannot miss the importance of "the name" as

The Holy Spirit is the personal, generating power of your transformation.

185

an invitation to being known, an invitation to intimacy and oneness. Jesus expresses His mission as "making Your name known."

The Spirit's mission to reveal the ways of Father and Son to us by convicting, convincing, teaching, and guiding us into all truth. The Holy Spirit is the transformation agent. The Spirit calibrates us to an understanding of what Father, Son, and Spirit are up to in filling the earth with the knowledge of the Lord. He knows how to connect us supernaturally with people, for the purpose of making the Kingdom available and bringing many sons to glory.

Questions:

1) What stood out to you as the most important idea of "the Missionary God."

2) How does this chapter reveal the Father as a missionary? What is His mission?

3) How does this chapter reveal the Son as a missionary to the world? What is His mission?

4) How has the Holy Spirit been sent into the world? What is the Spirit doing on mission?

The Holy Spirit is the personal, generating power of your transformation.

5) What does this mean for us as sons of God? What does it look like for you personally?

6) What is the significance of the Father making Himself known by His names (see the Supplemental Article)?

• •

Supplemental Article

Making His Name Known

In the most revealing and revelational prayer recorded in history, Jesus prayed for Himself, His disciples, and for all believers in John, chapter 17, (the end of His Last Supper discourse). It is often misinterpreted as a prayer for unity among believers, but is really about believers coming to realization of their sonship by oneness in the Triune relationship of Father, Son and Holy Spirit. This is the mission.

Jesus boldly declares in His open conversation to the Father, "I have finished the work You have given me to do" (John 17:4). This is the first priority of every son—via fellowship with the Father, the Son

finishes the Father's unfinished business. He declares that His business is to introduce orphaned humanity to the Father, and to give them eternal life (the Life of the Eternal One, life as God has it). John 17:3, 4 says:

You have given Him authority over all flesh, that He should give eternal life to as many as You have given Him. And this is eternal life, that they may know You, the only true God, and Jesus Christ whom You have sent. I have glorified You on the earth. I have finished the work

The Holy Spirit is the personal, generating power of your transformation.

*which You have given Me
to do.*

But something stands out to the casual reader that seems important to Jesus, referenced five times in His prayer. Jesus talks about manifesting the Father's name, keeping His disciples through the Name, and making the Father known by declaring His name.

- I have manifested Your name (v. 6)
- Keep them through Your name (v. 11)
- I have kept them in Your name (v. 12)
- Father, the world has not known You ... but these have known that you sent Me, and I have declared to them Your name. (vv. 25-26).

Biblically, names are significant for several reasons: it could record some aspects of a person's birth (e.g. causing pain), it expresses the parents' reaction to the birth of the child, the name can secure the solidarity of family ties, it can communicate God's message (e.g. Israel–having power with God), it can establish an affiliation with God (e.g. Abram to Abraham–inserting "Jah" in the name), or a prophetic declaration of the child's characteristics or purpose (e.g. "His name shall be called Jesus, for He shall save His people from their sin"). Often new names were given, replacing older names, to indicate a new beginning or new direction

in a person's life (e.g. Cephas becomes Peter). But Jesus points to another significant purpose.

Invitation to Intimacy

God revealed Himself progressively through history by covenant names; *Jehovah Jireh, Nissi, Tsidkenuh, Rapha, Shammah, Shalom*, etc. Each of these revealed more than simply how God acted—it revealed Who God is by nature (therefore, we can know He will act consistent to His nature). These names were given at pivotal encounter moments in history when God reveals Himself to others as an invitation to know Him in a new way that He had not been known before.

Think about the difference between meeting someone who simply shakes your hand—and someone who shakes your hand and gives you their name—"Hello, my name is Kerry. It's good to meet you." The one who offers their name is granting an invitation to be known—a conversational loop is opened by the giving of a name so that the other can call on them. It is inviting mutual self-disclosure. I am telling you something about myself, and I invite you to tell me something about yourself. When you shake someone's hand and give them your name, you pause, waiting for them to give you their name in return. The person that does not offer their name, whether intentional or not, doesn't invite further conversation.

The Holy Spirit is the personal, generating power of your transformation.

God has been inviting humanity into a deeper and deeper place of knowing by introducing Himself to us in new ways, by new names. And Jesus is very clear to declare His own coming is not just another name for God—but the highest name that opens the great gates to the love of the Father Himself. "I have declared to them Your name and will [continue to] declare it [through them], that the love with which You loved Me may be in them, and I in them" (John 17:26).

Jesus is the Father's handshake, His personal introduction to the world—much more than a business card; He's a personal gift.

A few years ago, at a pivotal moment in my own life, the Lord said to me, "Kerry, if you will tell me the secrets of your heart, I will tell you the secrets of Mine." This is what the Spirit of the Lord has come to do—*The Abba Formation*—to open our heart to the Father, and to disclose the deep thing of the Father to us. And the Spirit has given us another name—whereby we—as sons—cry *Abba*, Father. This *Abba* cry is not just about warm fuzzies, as nice as those are, but about empowering sons to finish the Father's unfinished business by an invitation—by making His name known in all the earth.

• •

Personal Reflection

What is the Lord saying to you?

The Holy Spirit is the personal, generating power of your transformation.

189

The Holy Spirit is the personal, generating power of your transformation.

Week 10
The Purpose of Transformation

Meditation Verse

> *[Jesus], though he was in the form of God, did not count equality with God a thing to be grasped. (Philippians 2:6, ESV)*

The verse in context:

> *Do nothing from selfish ambition or conceit, but in humility count others more significant than yourselves. Let each of you look not only to his own interests, but also to the interests of others. Have this mind among yourselves, which is yours in Christ Jesus, who, though he was in the form of God, did not count equality with God a thing to be grasped, but emptied himself, by taking the form of a servant, being born in the likeness of men. And being found in human form, he humbled himself by becoming obedient to the point of death, even death on a cross.*
>
> Philippians 2:3-8

Assigned Reading: *The Abba Formation*, Chapter 10

Chapter Summary

The gifts of the Spirit are free, but not automatically passed down from generation to generation. We must be intentional to apprehend the things of God for ourselves and for others.

Through Jesus, we have direct access to God and can know God personally. In Jesus' discourse (recorded in John 13-17) we see that sons are bold to take advantage of their direct access to the Father. The Father and Son come to us by the presence of the Holy Spirit and manifest themselves to us (John 14:18, 21, 23). Our responsibility is to make room for His Presence by cultivating a time, a place, and a way to meet with God. Traditionally these processes have been called spiritual disciplines. I call them "encounter triggers"—we put ourselves regularly in a position to encounter God, but it is never a ritual or "work" that earns us any favors.

Sons understand both the importance of staying full of the Spirit daily and the role that spiritual language can play in that ongoing fullness. As we mature in sonship the Father resources His sons and daughters supernaturally to carry on the ministry of Jesus. Sons understand that we are to continue the ministry of Jesus—the same works, and greater works, by the same Spirit—of healing and wholeness, and connecting people to the Father.

The Holy Spirit is the personal, generating power of your transformation.

Finally, God fills us with His love so that we, like Jesus, are moved with compassion. The ultimate purpose of our transformation is to connect orphans back to the Father.

Questions:

Look at John 13-17 and see how Jesus teaches His disciples that they will have direct access to the Father after the Spirit comes:

1) What are some ways listed that we can "cultivate" access to the Father?

2) How does Jesus teach His disciples in John 14 and 16 that staying filled with the Spirit? Why does He say it is of daily importance?

3) What do you do that has been most effective in staying filled with the Spirit?

4) How does Jesus tell His disciples in John 14 that He intends us to carry on His ministry?

The Holy Spirit is the personal, generating power of your transformation.

5) Think about (and share) one of your own stories of how you have connected others to God.

• •

Supplemental Article

Transformation: An Experience in Participation

The transforming work of the Spirit—*The Abba Formation*—displaces old ways of thinking and believing by an inside out process. We "grow up into Him", that is, the life and love of Jesus is fills our spirit (the inner man, the hidden man of the heart) by the Holy Spirit via the new birth. But our minds must come to know by renewal what our spirits became by regeneration. The person that is born again, alive to God, born of the Spirit, now has a new way of knowing. Not only does the believer live in two world's simultaneously, but has two ways of knowing, two ways of seeing, two ways of hearing—one is natural (and tuned to the natural world), and one is spiritual (and tuned to the spirit world). This new way of knowing by the S/spirit is described by the use of the New Testament Greek word *epiginōskō*—to know.

Our minds can take in information about something observed, but there is a huge difference between knowing about something/someone and knowing someone intimately and experientially. Most "romantic languages" have words that convey the distinction between knowing about a person or thing, and intimately knowing that person. In the Greek language "*oida*" is the word used to know about something (e.g. to know Scriptures in the Bible, celebrities on TV, or a good cooking recipe)—"to have knowledge of a thing." The word *ginōskō* gets closer; meaning to have some relationship between the subject and the object known. I can really "love" a good book, a great hamburger, or a sports team. There is a relationship, but it is a subject-to-object relationship, not a person-to-person relationship. In Spanish the words are *saber* and *conocer*.

When Paul refers to "the knowledge of God" (Phil. 3:8; Eph. 1:17; 2 Cor. 4:6) or Peter refers to "the knowledge the Lord Jesus

The Holy Spirit is the personal, generating power of your transformation.

Christ" (2 Pet. 1:8; 2:20), they both use the word *epiginōskō*.

The formal definition is "to fully perceive" and implies a relationship between the knower and the known. The word suggests an advanced knowledge; a special participation and relationship. In 1 Timothy 4:3, the phrase, "them that believe and know (*epiginōsko*) the truth," reflects an experienced participation with the truth. This kind of knowledge "perfectly unites the subject with the object.[10]

You can't have a relationship with abstract truth or with a book. But you can have a relationship with the Spirit of Truth. The reason is because one is the work of the head, the other is the work of the heart (spirit of man, where the Holy Spirit lives).

Information is not the same as transformation. Even good cognitive thinking is trapped inside a particular culture, our education, our social and family conditioning. It means that with all our knowing we must carry a humility of "knowing that I do not know." That I know things in my spirit of which my mind can't catch up; allowing God to fill in all the gaps in an "unspeakable" way. The Enlightenment espoused reason and empirical scientific data as the only reality. Unfortunately, Western Christianity wanted to match the new rationalism with what felt like solid knowing, and we mimicked the secular mind instead of what Paul calls "knowing spiritual things in a spiritual

way" (1 Corinthians 2:13). We forsook the inner world of the spirit—*epiginōskō* knowing—and settled for *oida*, knowing about God (think systematic theology and doctrine), rather than living into the mystery of life with the Eternal One. We've settled for a knowledge of God that is dead, powerless, and only available to highly educated.

We've settled for a form of worship that settles for expository line-by-line preaching, but shuns the demonstration of the Spirit's power.

The old-fashioned biblical word of this kind of knowing is faith. Faith is being convinced of a reality that you cannot see. Faith is a kind of knowing that doesn't need physical certainty, yet doesn't dismiss that kind of knowledge either. As Paul says, "While we look not at things which are seen, but at things which are not seen. For the things which are seen are temporary, but the things which are not seen are eternal" (2 Cor. 4:18). It is a knowing by participation with—instead of an observation of .... It is knowing subject-to-subject instead of subject-to-object.

This kind of knowing is by the Holy Spirit in your own spirit; it is experiential, and participative. This kind of transformation does not primarily come from a book, but by a personal experience with the Holy Spirit which generates a breakthrough in your awareness of who God is (the knowledge of

The Holy Spirit is the personal, generating power of your transformation.

God) and something of your own freedom as a son of His (the power that is at work in us who believe).

Why is the Presence of God so important? Why do we need to cultivate "encounter triggers" (spiritual disciplines) to continually put ourselves in a place to hear His voice? Why is biblical meditation, prayer, prayer language, worship so important to our transformation? Because these open our spirit to a kind of knowing and transformation unattainable through the processes of the mind.

---

[13]Ed. Geoffrey Bromley. *Theological Dictionary of the New Testament. One Volume Abridged.* Eerdmans. (119-121).

• •

Personal Reflection

What is the Lord saying to you?

The Holy Spirit is the personal, generating power of your transformation.

The Holy Spirit is the personal, generating power of your transformation.

Week 11

You Say You Want a Revolution

Meditation Verse

> *For the weapons of our warfare are not carnal but mighty in God for pulling down strongholds, casting down arguments and every high thing that exalts itself against the knowledge of God. (2 Corinthians 10:4-5)*

The verse in context:

> *For though we walk in the flesh, we do not war according to the flesh. For the weapons of our warfare are not carnal but mighty in God for pulling down strongholds, casting down arguments and every high thing that exalts itself against the knowledge of God, bringing every thought into captivity to the obedience of Christ, and being ready to punish all disobedience when your obedience is fulfilled.*
>
> 2 Corinthians 10:3-6

Assigned Reading: *The Abba Formation*, Chapter 11

Chapter Summary

Jesus came to the earth and was clothed in humanity to start, not a new religion, but a revolution of sonship. He came to affect a radical restoration of sons to the Father. He came to turn the hearts of fathers to the children and children to fathers—more specifically, to turn the hearts of orphans to the Father.

One of the primary rules of revolutionaries is to redefine existing terms. Jesus reinterpreted Moses, the Law, the commandments, rabbinical ministry, and the understanding of the terms "holy," "clean," "unclean" and "common."

One of the keys to our own spiritual transformation is our willingness to have truth and reality redefined. The work of the Spirit is to redefine our view of God and ourselves as Father and sons. This is *The Abba Formation*. Personal transformation is not just for personal comfort, but to be free to be other-centered. Any way that we bring the reality of the Spirit dimension into this physical realm, we have brought the eternal into the temporal, and made the Father's love available to others. We can do this with our words, with our actions, and with our interactions with others.

The Holy Spirit is the personal, generating power of your transformation.

For Jesus, this has always been a global mission. His desire has always been to fill the whole earth with the knowledge of the glory of the Lord, and He is doing this by giving His Spirit to sons and daughters.

Questions:

1) In what ways could we say Jesus was a revolutionary toward the religious establishment of His day? Why did the Pharisees hate Him as they did?

2) In what ways did Jesus redefine the terms of relationship with God, as the Jewish people in that day had come to know Him?

3) How is "keeping (*tereō*: cherishing, watching over, guarding) the commandments" different in the New Covenant than under the Older Covenant?

4) Why is the penetration of the spiritual realm into the natural realm so important for bringing orphans back to the Father?

5) What are some of the ways we can "poke a hole" in the seeming separation, to make the Kingdom of Heaven available now?

The Holy Spirit is the personal, generating power of your transformation.

6) What stood out to you from the supplemental reading?

• •

Supplemental Article

Quiet Times Don't Have to Be Quiet

I'm not sure where the term "quiet time" came from; perhaps as far back as the mystics of the mid-centuries, I suppose. I get the image of monks walking quietly, solemnly through dark corridors of a monastery or cathedral. No talking is allowed, perhaps a Gregorian chant is being sung in a great hall a few rooms away. Perhaps the notion that the physical body is evil and our natural desires (such as communication) must be suppressed so the spiritual senses can gain ascendancy are behind the idea of quiet time. It seems to promote an assumption that it is really hard to hear God's voice, so we must silence everything else.

Clearly, we must respect the need to put the Father's voice as preeminent in our lives. Jesus modeled this priority by withdrawing from the crowds, and even His own disciples, rising early in the morning to spend time with His Father (Mark 1:35). If Jesus needed that time, can we survive spiritually without it? No.

But I do want to press on the idea of "quiet time."

What we call a daily quiet time is a meeting between a disciple and the Lord Jesus. It should not be impromptu, but strategic and as consistent as possible. We can commune with the Lord moment by moment as we go through the day with the goal to stay in constant communication—as Paul said, to pray without ceasing (1 Thess. 5:17). But we should also have those times each day that we set aside solely for the purpose of communing with God.

Your time with the Lord should usually include several ingredients that may not be so quiet. When Jesus teaches His disciples to pray, He begins with worship. "*Abba* in heaven, holy is Your name." That's worship. You should consider available tools (that will not be too distracting) to open your heart and provides an easy on-ramp into worship. Sometimes I will pull out my guitar and play some familiar choruses that are intentionally vertical. By vertical I mean it is

---

The Holy Spirit is the personal, generating power of your transformation.

personal conversation between me and God. I'm singing to Him not just about Him. I'm using the personal pronouns "you" and "me" more than "he" and "they" or "them." David, as a worshiper of God, gave us huge clues as to how to enter into the presence of the Lord, "I will enter his gates with thanksgiving and my heart, I will enter his courts with praise" (Ps. 100:4).

Worship allows me to position myself in a proper perspective as creation under the Creator. I lift up my voice, I sing to Him. I tell him how much I love Him. I acknowledge that He is God and I'm His creation; He is the shepherd and I am the sheep of his pasture (Ps. 100:3). This opens my heart, and the windows of my soul, to connect with Him—and it may not be very quiet. After I've connected with God audibly. I will engage my body by lifting my hands, or kneeling on the floor, or simply bowing my head.

Years ago, my mentor and spiritual father, Pastor Jack Hayford, taught a simple way to think about approaching my times with God. He used the acronym of the word P.R.A.I.S.E. Perhaps it will help you as well.

Present. I present myself to God when I first wake up in the morning. I will audibly say, "*Abba*, I belong to you. I love you. Here I am. I come before You today to open my heart to You and ask You to open Your heart to me. That doesn't sound too profound.

It's not. It is simply turning my attention to Him (usually before I get downstairs to the coffeemaker).

Raise. I raise my hands. This is not a sign of being charismatic, this is a sign of surrender, reaching, yearning, dependent, and longing to connect with Him. What I know is that my flesh wars against the things of the S/spirit. So, every morning I will use my physical body to make a move toward God. For me, it is simply the lifting of my hands. David said, "May the lifting of my hands be as the evening sacrifice" (Ps. 141:2). He knew that God would receive a simple physical act as a spiritual sacrificial gift.

Affirm. I affirm that He is God and I'm His child. I will acknowledge out loud that He is the creator and I'm His creation I will say audibly, "*Abba*, you have made us and not we ourselves. I am the sheep of Your pasture. I need to hear Your voice today. And I'm confident that I, as your sheep, know Your voice and will hear it today. I affirm that You have saved me, that Your Spirit lives in me, and that by Your Spirit I can hear Your voice today."

Invite. I invite the Lord to come speak to me by His Spirit. I will do this audibly. It's the way I pray. I will say, "*Abba*, I belong to you. Everything I have is Yours. I invite You to come reveal yourself to me today. Speak to me today.

The Holy Spirit is the personal, generating power of your transformation.

Fill me with Your Spirit today. Father, I want everything that You have for me because I know that every good and perfect gift comes from you" (James 1:17). I also speak to the Holy Spirit within me and I say, "Holy Spirit, I invite You to rise up within me and reveal what the Father has revealed to You about me, for me, and what You want to do through me today" (1 Cor. 2:10).

Sing. There are many commands and exhortations in the Scriptures to sing to the Lord. We are commanded to sing unto the Lord a new song, and to sing psalms, hymns and spiritual songs (Ps. 96:1; 98:1; Eph. 5:18; Col. 3:25). I notice that the Scriptures don't direct me to find someone who can sing really well to sing in my place. The Scriptures invite me to sing—raspy, warbley voice and all—to the Lord.

By the time I have presented myself to the Lord, lifted my hands, affirmed that He is God and I'm his child, invited Him to come speak to me, and sing to Him, I have my coffee in my hand and I'm ready to engage with his Living (Logos), spoken (*rhema*), and written (*graphe*) Word. Just before I open the Scriptures I will begin to express Thanksgiving.

Express. By expressing thanksgiving I'm putting my heart in a positive "attitude of gratitude" and receptivity. I am not approaching God with a laundry list of problems, petitions, or needs that have to be met. I'm worshiping Him. I'm singing to Him. I'm expressing Thanksgiving first for who He is and then for what He has done. This puts me in a place to hear Him speaking to me about the "who," not just the "what." Our tendency is to ask God questions about our daily lives; to gather info about the whys and the hows. But God wants to speak to us about who we are in the context of who He is. God wants to release purpose, and destiny, and glory in our lives, and information rarely does this.

As I'm reading the Scriptures, usually in my One Year Bible, I turn what I am reading into a conversation. "Father, do You see any of that in me? What are You saying to me through this story? I see this leader, and that leader, falling short of Your plan; what do You want to say to me through this passage?" Invariably, that conversation turns into what we call intercessory prayer. I will be praying for my children, my church, the men I'm discipling, and those things that I have heard the Lord speaking to me. I listen and write what I hear. By the way, always, always have a journal and a writing instrument handy, ready to write what you hear. If you approach the Father expecting to hear, you are half way there.

Can you see why this could be called a "Focus Time," or a "Daily Appointment," but perhaps not a quiet time.

The Holy Spirit is the personal, generating power of your transformation.

Your "focus time" with God will not always look or feel the same way. But there are certain ingredients that will keep your relationship with Him alive and fresh. Your time should include worship and singing, reading the Scriptures, conversations with the living Christ as a result of the Scriptures, taking a significant phrase as your meditation for the day, and responsive prayer. These components will be the focus of our supplemental reading in the weeks to come.

Personal Reflection

What is the Lord saying to you?

The Holy Spirit is the personal, generating power of your transformation.

Congratulations!
You have completed

The Abba
JOURNEY

Remember that Jesus told us to "go into all the world and make disciples of all nations" (Matthew 28:19). Consider inviting two other friends to join you on *The Abba Journey*. Form a triad and lead them through the journey.

Let's fulfill the Great Commission together!

We hope you have experienced, and agree with us that the optimal approach for personal transformation is in triads—three people studying, journeying, and growing together. An effective triad is comprised of three key components:

1. **The presence of the Lord,** starting each triad gathering with worship and prayer
2. **The truth**, which comes through the content of the books
3. **Relationships**, which comes through your weekly time together.

Read a chapter, answer the questions at the end of each chapter, then meet to worship, pray, discuss your discoveries, and minister to one another.

The *Abba* Journey:

Part 1: *The Abba Foundation: Knowing the Father Through the Eyes of Jesus*, by Chiqui Wood. Burkhart Books, 2018. ISBN: 978-1-940359601

Part 2: *The Abba Factor: Seeing Yourself Through the Eyes of the Father*, by Kerry Wood. Burkhart Books, 2018. ISBN: 978-1-940359-61-8

Part 3: *The Abba Formation: The Holy Spirit's Role in Your Personal Transformation*, by Kerry Wood. Burkhart Books, 2018. ISBN: 978-1-940359656.

About the Authors

Kerry Wood is passionate about authentic Christianity lived in the power of the Spirit. In over thirty-five years of pastoral ministry he has focused on the local church, prayer movements, and community transformation initiatives. He has launched or sponsored several church plants in the U.S. and abroad and has spoken in leadership conferences, crusades, and local churches in more than twenty countries and throughout the U.S. He has authored a variety of ministry materials, published articles, Bible curricula, and audio-video teaching.

As a local church leader, seminary professor and member of the Society of Pentecostal Studies, Kerry is committed to partnership with Holy Spirit, intercessory prayer, teaching the Word, five-fold equipping of the Church, leadership development and church planting. He endeavors to steward partnership with the Holy Spirit through the gifts, and introducing people to Spirit Baptism. His philosophy of life and ministry is about "being before doing," an overflow of God's fullness as the source of all activity.

Kerry holds a Doctor of Ministry (Jack W. Hayford Chancellor's Outstanding Graduate) and Master of Divinity from The King's University (Los Angeles), a Masters of Arts in Biblical Literature from the Assemblies of God Theological Seminary, and Bachelors in Christian Ministry from Southwestern Assemblies of God University.

Ana Isabel "Chiqui" Polo-Wood was raised in Bogotá, Colombia, in the home of Pedro Polo and Alicia Fonnegra. She came to know Jesus as Lord and savior at age 15, and over the last 30 years has served in many areas of ministry including Teacher, Mentor, Associate Pastor, and Director of Adult Education. God has given her many opportunities to travel to several other nations to preach, train teachers and help local Church leaders start Leadership Institutes for their congregations. She lives in Texas with her husband, Kerry. They love ministering together both locally and abroad.

Chiqui is passionate for the Word and the presence of God, and continually amazed at the realization that the Triune God has chosen to partner with humanity to establish His Kingdom on earth. Her desire and goal in ministry is to see the Body of Christ fully equipped to live in the fullness of life that the Father has prepared for His children.

Chiqui earned her Master of Divinity (Outstanding Scholar) and Doctor of Ministry from The King's University, Los Angeles, California in 2011 and 2014 respectively. In addition, she is the author of the book, *Lessons Learned in the Battle*.

To learn more about Kerry and Chiqui's ministry and resources visit:

www.DrKerryWood.com,
www.ChiquiPoloWood.com
www.TableOfFriends.com

Check out the other books by Kerry & Chiqui:

- *The Gifts of the Spirit for a New Generation* by Dr. Kerry Wood
- *Lessons Learned in the Battle: How to Live in Victory No Matter What* by Dr. Chiqui Wood

Made in the USA
Middletown, DE
28 September 2023

39657805R00115